D1338415

The Observer's Books

THE OBSERVER'S BOOK OF

TREES

Compiled by

W. J. STOKOE

Describing
ONE HUNDRED AND SIX SPECIES
with 50 line illustrations, 12 colour plates
and 110 half tone photographs

FREDERICK WARNE & CO. LTD.
FREDERICK WARNE & CO. INC.
LONDON · NEW YORK

SBN 7232 0046 7

*Printed in Great Britain by
Butler & Tanner Ltd., Frome and London*

1505.2569

PREFACE

This little volume, specially designed for the pocket, is not, of course, intended to be an addition to the numerous works upon sylviculture and forestry, but a straightforward attempt to assist the observer and nature-lover to an easy and ready means for identifying the trees that abound, almost everywhere, in our land, and in the earnest hope that it will create an interest sufficient to encourage a more serious and deeper study of the sylva of our countryside.

Although the list of those species which are generally considered to be indigenous to the British Islands is a very short one, it has here been supplemented by the inclusion and description of certain exotic trees that have long been naturalized in our woods, together with some of foreign origin, introduced so long ago that they are now commonly regarded as native by those who are not botanists.

In describing the various species, technical terms have been purposely avoided as far as possible, whilst, at the same time, the necessary details to enable the observer to identify the trees quickly have been carefully maintained.

The illustrations given of the tree and bole, together with the coloured plates and text figures, show at a glance the general character of the form, foliage, and in most cases, the flower and fruit also, which should prove additional aids to identification.

Extracts have been taken from the standard work "Wayside and Woodland Trees," by Edward Step, F.L.S., published by Frederick Warne & Co., Ltd. Thanks are given to Henry Irving for the use of photographs reproduced on pages 22, 25, 29, 35, 36, 38, 44, 49, 50, 59, 61, 63, 64, 67, 71, 75, 79, 83, 88, 94, 95, 101, 102, 105, 109, 113, 117, 121, 125, 129, 136, 137, 142, 147, 151, 153, 155, 157, 162, 169, 174, 176, 177, 180, 185, 188, 189, 191, 192, 194, 197, 198, 200, 205, 209, 213, 217 and 220; to Harold Bastin for photographs on pages 37, 43, 52, 55, 57, 58, 60, 78, 91, 104, 112, 128, 135, 152, 154, 159, 179, 193, 208, 212 and 216; to Eric J. Hosking, F.R.P.S., for photographs on pages 21, 24, 31, 41, 99, 108, 116, 120, 124, 132, 139, 141, 145, 156, 168, 178, 184, 200, 204, 219 and 222; to Maurice Nimmo for photographs on pages 28, 34, 66, 70, 74, 81, 86 and 173; to J. E. Downward, F.I.B.P., for photographs on pages 46 and 164; and to Gerald Atkinson for the photograph on page 22. Thanks are also given to Mable E. Step for line drawings illustrating the leaves, flowers and fruits; and to R. Neil Chrystal, M.A., D.Sc., for the description of *Liriodendron tulipifera*.

INTRODUCTION

There are two points of view from which to regard trees—the mercantile and the aesthetic. The former is well exemplified in Dumbiedike's advice to Jock: "Jock, when ye hae naething else to do, ye may be aye sticking in a tree; it will be growing, Jock, when ye're sleeping." The careful Scot was thinking of the "unearned increment" another generation might gather in, due to the almost unceasing activity of the vegetable cells in the manufacture of timber. The other view was expressed by the "Autocrat of the Breakfast-table" in a letter to a friend: "Whenever we plant a tree we are doing what we can to make our planet a more wholesome and happier dwelling place for those who come after us, if not for ourselves." But, after all, it is the trees that have been planted by Nature that give the greatest pleasure apart from commercial considerations— the lonely Pine, that grows in rugged grandeur on the edge of the escarpment where its seed was planted in the crevice by the wind; the Oak that grows outside the forest, where a squirrel or a jay dropped the acorn, and where the young tree had room all its life to throw out its arms as it would; the little cluster of Birches that springs from the ferns and moss of the hillside. All trees so grown develop an individuality that is not apparent in their fellows of the timber forest; and however we may delight in the peace and quiet of the forest, with its softened light and cool fragrant air, we can there only regard the trees in a mass.

Nature and the timber-producer have different aims and pursue different methods in the making of forests. Nature mixes her seeds and sows them broadcast over the land she intends to turn into a forest, that the more vigorous kinds may act as nurses, sheltering and protecting the less robust. Then comes the struggle for existence, with its final ending in the survival of the fittest.

In the meantime the mixed forest has given shelter to an enormous population—plants, animals, birds, and insects—and has been a delightful recreation ground for man.

The timber-producer aims at so controlling the struggle for existence that the survival of the fit is maintained from start to finish. He plants his young trees in regular order, putting in nurses at intervals and along the borders, intending to cut them down when his purpose has been served. The timber-trees are allowed no elbow-room, the lateral branches are discouraged, and steady upward growth and the production of " canopy " is abetted. His aim is to get them as nearly alike as possible, with the minimum of difference in girth at top and bottom of each bole. This means a thicker and longer balk of clean timber when the tree is felled and squared. The continuous canopy induces growth in the upward direction only, and discourages the weeds and undergrowth that add to the charm of the forest, but which unprofitably use up the wood-producing elements of the soil.

The greater the success of the forester, the more profound is the solemn stillness of the forest—

and the more monotonous. In place of the natural forest, with its varied and teeming life, we have what Wordsworth called a " timber factory." In the natural forest, with its mixture of many kinds of trees, the undergrowth of shrubs, the carpet of grass and weeds, the stronger trees spread out their arms in all directions, and fritter away (as the forester would say) their wood-producing powers in making much firewood and little valuable timber. But the result is very beautiful, and the nature-lover can wander among it without tiring, and can study without exhausting its treasures.

With every desire that the natural resources of our country should be properly developed, it is sincerely hoped that a few of the woods and wastes of Nature's own planting will be left for the recreation of all those who have not yet taken to appraising the value of everything by the price it will fetch in the market.

The trees described in this volume are the really wild growths that have lived a natural life; and though many of the illustrations are from planted trees, they are such as have been allowed to grow as they would, and show the character-istic habit of the species.

A few words on the life of a tree may be wel-comed here by those readers who have not made a study of botany.

Almost every tree in its natural habitat produces seeds and is reproduced by them. The flowering of our forest trees is a phenomenon that does not, as a rule, attract attention, but their fruiting or seed-bearing becomes apparent to all who visit the woods in autumn.

9

A tree has lived many years before it is capable of producing seed. The seed-bearing age is different in each species; thus, the Oak begins to bear when it is between sixty and seventy years old, the Ash between forty and fifty, the Birch and Sweet Chestnut at twenty-five years. Some produce seed every year after that period is reached, others every second, third or fifth year; others, again, bear fitfully except at intervals of from six to nine years, when they produce an enormous crop.

Most tree-seeds germinate in the spring following their maturity, but they are not all distributed when ripe. The Birch, the Elm and the Aspen, for examples, disperse their seeds in spring, and these germinate soon after they have been shed.

The seeds contain sufficient nutriment to feed the seedling whilst it is developing its roots and first real leaves. We can, of course, go further back in starting our observations of the life progress of the monarch of the forest. We can dissect the insignificant greenish flower of the Oak when the future seed (acorn) is but a single cell, a tiny bag filled with protoplasm.

From that early stage to the period when the tree is first ripe for conversion into timber, we span a hundred and fifty years, equal to two good human lives, and the Oak is but at the point where a man attains his majority. The Oak is built up after the fashion by which man attains to his full stature. It is a process of multiplication of weak, minute cells, which become specialized for distinct offices in the economy of the vegetable community we call a tree. Some go to renew and enlarge the roots, others to the perfecting of that system of vessels through which the crude fluids from the roots are carried up to the topmost leaf, whence, after undergoing chemical transformation in the leaf laboratory, it is circulated to all parts of the organism to make possible the production of more cells. Each of these has a special task, and it becomes invested with cork or wood to enable it to become part of the bark or the timber; or it remains soft and develops the green colouring matter, which enables it, when exposed to sunlight, to manufacture starch from carbon-dioxide and water.

This is very similar to what takes place in the human organism, where the nutriment taken in is used up in the production of new cells, which are differentiated into muscle-cells, bone-cells, epidermal cells, and so forth, building up or renewing muscles or nerves, bones or arteries; but the mechanism of distribution is different, the heart-pump doing the work of capillary attraction and gravitation.

The tree, as we have indicated, gets its food from the air and the soil. The rootlets have the power of absorbing the dissolved mineral salts in the soil in which they ramify. They are often helped materially in this respect—so far as organic matter is concerned, such as the breaking up of dead leaves—by a fungus that invests them with a mantle of delicate threads known as mycorrhiza; so that the fluid that is taken up by the roots is not merely water, but water plus dissolved mineral matter and nitrogen. At the same time as the roots are thus absorbing liquid nutriment, the leaves, pierced with thousands of little *stomata*, or mouths, take in atmospheric air, containing oxygen, carbon-dioxide and water vapour. The leaf-cells containing the green colouring matter (*chlorophyll*) by the energy of the sun seize hold of the carbon-dioxide and release the oxygen. The carbon-dioxide is then combined with water to form food materials. These are circulated for the sustenance of all the organs and tissues.

The flowering of the trees varies so greatly that it can only be dealt with satisfactorily as each species is described. It may be stated, however, that all true forest trees are wind fertilized, and therefore have inconspicuous greenish blossoms. By true forest trees we mean those that alone or slightly mixed are capable of forming high forest. The smaller trees such as the Crab, Rowan, Cherry, Blackthorn, Hawthorn, Buckthorn, etc., belong more to the open woodland, to the common, and the hedgerow. These from their habitat can be seen singly, and therefore can make use of the conspicuous flowers that are fertilized by insects.

CLASSIFIED INDEX

FAMILIES, GENERA AND SPECIES

IDENTIFICATION BY TWIGS AND BUDS

The following section has been drawn up to assist the student to identify any common tree at a time when foliage distinctions are unavailable.

Tulip Tree (p. 21)

Buds compressed greyish, with two valvate scales.

Lime (p. 24)

Twigs red, zig-zag, glabrous, shining.

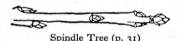

Spindle Tree (p. 31)

Twigs sage green.

Purging Buckthorn (p. 34)

Bud scales glabrous, branches with spines.

Horse Chestnut (p. 37)

Buds large, up to 1 inch long, sticky.

IDENTIFICATION BY TWIGS AND BUDS

Field Maple (p. 41)

Bud scales hairy at the tips, branches without spines ; older twigs with corky ridges.

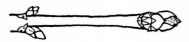

Sycamore (p. 43)

Bud scales yellowish-green with dark brown markings.

Norwav Maple (p. 45)

Bud scales pinkish or yellowish-brown.

Laburnum (p. 46)

Twigs greyish-green ; exposed bud scales about 4 with silvery-haired scales.

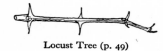

Locust Tree (p. 49)

Bundle traces three, leaf scars with a membrane, twigs spiny.

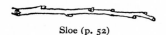

Sloe (p. 52)

Twigs spiny, buds very small, round.

Wild Cherry (p. 57)

Twigs not spiny, buds large, glossy, ovoid with about 6 exposed scales.

IDENTIFICATION BY TWIGS AND BUDS

Wild Pear (p. 60)

Twigs yellowish-brown, buds acute.

Wild Apple (p. 63)

Young twigs partially hairy, short branches ending in a thorn.

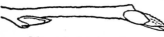

Whitebeam (p. 66)

Buds elongated, hairy at the tips.

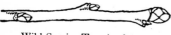

Wild Service Tree (p. 69)

Buds sub-globose, smooth at the tips.

Mountain Ash (p. 70)

Buds woolly, scales dark purple.

Hawthorn (p. 78)

Twigs greyish, spiny, buds minute, rounded.

Dogwood (p. 81)

Twigs smooth, glabrous, blood-red in colour.

IDENTIFICATION BY TWIGS AND BUDS

Elder (p. 83)

Bud scales loosely arranged, pith wide, spongy.

Guelder Rose (p. 86)

Bud scales greenish-yellow; young twigs longitudinally ridged.

Wayfaring Tree (p. 88)

Twigs mealy.

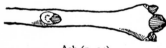

Ash (p. 94)

Bud scales black, terminal bud the largest; twigs smooth.

English Elm (p. 108)

Buds blackish red, ovoid, subacute. Twigs hairy or glabrous.

Plane (p. 112)

Buds large, conical, enclosed by a single glossy conical scale.

Walnut (p. 116)

Pith chambered; bundle traces in three compound groups.

Birch (p. 120)

Exposed bud scales two or three, twigs slender, flexible, often warty.

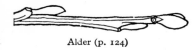

Alder (p. 124)

Buds stalked, with waxy bloom, twigs reddish brown.

Hornbeam (p. 128)

Twigs as above but buds ovoid, shorter.

Hazel (p. 132)

Buds pale brown, obtuse twigs often clothed with glandular bristles.

English Oak (p. 135)

Buds clustered at tip of shoot, with numerous 5-ranked scales.

Turkey Oak (p. 140)

Buds clustered, and invested with long narrow stipules.

Sweet Chestnut (p. 141)

Twigs reddish brown, longitudinally ridged, pith deeply grooved.

Beech (p. 145)

Twigs slender, buds spiky, spindle-shaped, spreading, $\frac{1}{2}$ inch or more long.

Crack Willow (p. 153)

Buds appressed to the twig, exposed bud scale, one.

White Poplar (p. 168)

Young twigs covered with a white, cottony film.

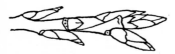

Black Poplar (p. 172)

Buds chestnut-brown, glossy, often resinous.

THE TULIP TREE

Family MAGNOLIACEAE   *Liriodendron tulipifera*

This species is widely, but not commonly, distributed in the Midlands and South of England, and some splendid specimens can be seen at Oxford, Reading, Tortworth, and other places.

The Tulip Trees are close relatives of the true Magnolias from which they differ in having their leaves truncate at the tips, and never pointed. *L. tulipifera* is an American species and was brought to England in the 17th century. In its

native haunts the tree attains a height of over 150 feet, and in this country specimens of over 100 feet in height are known.

The tree is much valued for its beautiful form and fine bole, and the bark of the roots and stem has a pleasant pungent scent. The wood is much used in North America and known as yellow poplar. It is smooth and of fine grain, not easily split and is suitable for interior work.

The leaves are very characteristic. They are saddle-shaped, with the apices always truncate and with a slender leaf-stalk two to four inches in length.

The flowers are produced in June and July and are tulip-shaped, which gives the tree its name. The oblong petals are greenish-white with an orange-coloured spot at the base, about one and a half inches long, erect and with the tips over-lapping. The numerous orange-yellow stamens are crowded around the large and pointed central pistil. The flowers, when picked and placed in a flat bowl, look just like small water-lilies.

Leaves and flower

The spectacle of a tulip tree in full flower is very striking, especially at night time, when the moonlight is on the flowers, giving the impression of the tree being illuminated. It is said to be one of the largest and finest trees of the North American forests, and it is to be regretted, there-fore, that this interesting species is not planted much more commonly in this country than it is, not only for its fine summer form and foliage, but also for its rich yellow autumnal tint.

THE LIME

There are three kinds of Lime in general cultivation in this country. They are the Large-leaved (*Tilia platyphyllos*), the Small-leaved (*T. cordata*), and the Common Lime (*T. vulgaris*). The last named is generally admitted to be a hybrid between the two preceding species, and is the one most commonly planted. The Small-leaved Lime, which does not occur in woods north of Cumberland, is now generally regarded as a true native, but there is no doubt as to the Large-leaved Lime, which is only growing really wild in the woods of Herefordshire, Radnorshire, and the West Riding of Yorkshire.

The Large-leaved Lime growing in parkland or meadow with its roots deep in good light loam attains a height of eighty or ninety feet, and the girth of such a specimen, four feet from the ground, would be about fifteen feet. Larger specimens have been recorded, up to twenty-seven feet in girth.

All our Limes have similar straight, tall stems, clad in smooth bark, and with a similar habit of growth. They demand genial climatic conditions for their development, consequently do not put forth their leaves until May. The period of their leafy state is comparatively short, for they lose their leaves early in the autumn.

The leaf is heart-shaped, with one of the basal lobes larger than the other, and the edges are cut into saw-like teeth.

The yellowish-white flower has distinct sepals and petals, an abundance of nectar, and a strong,

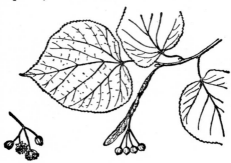

Leaves, flowers and fruits

sweet fragrance as of Honeysuckle. They are in clusters of six or seven, the stalks of all arising from one very long and stouter stalk, which is attached for half its length to a strap-shaped bract. They are not produced until the boughs are well clothed with leaves. Cross-fertilization is ensured by the innumerable bees that visit the flowers for the abundant nectar they contain, and which the bees convert into a first-rate honey.

The flowers are succeeded by globose little fruits, each about a quarter of an inch across, yellow and covered with pale down. In a good season these will be found to contain one or two seeds, but often, in this country, the summers are too short to ripen them. The Lime does not begin to bear until its thirty-fifth year, and its seed-crop depends entirely on the weather.

The question of its value as timber is probably rarely taken into account when it is planted in this country, where its ornamental appearance as an avenue or shade-tree is its great recommendation ; yet it serves for many smaller uses, where lightness and fine grain are required. It is largely used by the makers of musical instruments, and it is from the inner bark of the Lime that bast mats are made. It must also be mentioned that the wonderful carvings of Grinling Gibbons were executed in this wood. It is one of the long-lived trees, its full life-period being certainly five centuries.

Those in St. James's Park are popularly supposed to have been planted, at the suggestion of John Evelyn, somewhere about the year 1660. There is also a fine Lime avenue in Bushey Park probably planted by Dutch William. Lime avenues often include more than one species. The longest avenue of Limes is probably that on the Clumber estate in Nottinghamshire. It consists of 1,315 trees, planted in a double row on each side of the drive and is 1 mile and 1,590 yards long.

THE HOLLY

Family AQUIFOLIACEAE   *Ilex aquifolium*

The Holly is well distributed throughout the British Islands, and it is probable that no other tree is so well known.

It must be regarded as one of our small trees, although the record height is seventy-one feet, with a girth of four and a half feet.

28

THE HOLLY

The bark of the Holly is smooth and pale grey in colour. The leaves are oval in shape, of a leathery consistence, with a firmer margin, running out into long sharp spines. It is a fact worthy of note that when the Holly has attained a height of ten feet or so, it frequently clothes its upper branches in leaves that have no spines.

No doubt, in the early history of the Holly, cattle found out its good qualities as food, and browsed upon the then unarmed foliage. In self-defence the tree developed spines upon its leaves, and so kept its enemies at a distance. Above the reach of these marauders the production of spines would be a useless waste of material.

The small white flowers of the Holly are about a quarter of an inch across, with four petals and four to six stamens or two to four stigmas. Sometimes flowers with stamens are produced by the same tree that bears flowers with stigmas; but usually the male and female flowers are borne by separate trees, so the possessor of a Holly that is solely male is puzzled by the fact that his tree, though covered with blossom, never produces a berry.

The fruit is similar in structure to that of the Plum and Cherry and is termed a *drupe*; but

instead of the single stone of these fruits, in the Holly-berry there are two or more bony little stones, each with its contained seed. The berries ripen about September, and are then scarlet and glossy.

The wood of the Holly has an exceedingly fine grain, and is very hard and white, used often as a substitute for Box-wood, and, when dyed black, in lieu of Ebony.

THE SPINDLE TREE

Family CELASTRACEAE   *Euonymus europaeus*

The Spindle is indigenous throughout the British Islands, but cannot be said to be generally common ; it is rarer in Scotland and Ireland than in England.

The Spindle is right on the borderland between trees and shrubs, for though it will grow into a tree twenty feet high, yet our hedgerow specimens are usually bushlike and only ten or twelve feet high.

Until the autumn the Spindle might be confused with the Buckthorn and Dogwood, but its four-angled twigs should enable it to be easily recognized. In October its quaint fruits change to a

pale crimson hue, which renders them a conspicuous feature of a hedgerow.

The trunk of the Spindle is clothed in smooth grey bark. The twigs, which are in pairs, starting from opposite sides of a branch, are four-angled.

The shining leaves vary from egg-shaped to lance-shaped, with finely-toothed edges. They are arranged in pairs, and in autumn they change to yellow and red.

The small greenish-white flowers are borne in loose clusters, of the type known as *cymes*, from the axils of the leaves, and appear in May and June. Some contain both stamens and pistil, but others are either stamenate *or* pistillate. The calyx is cut into four or six parts, the petals and stamens agree with these parts in number, but the lobes of the stigma only range from three to five, corresponding with the cells of the ovary.

The fruit is deeply lobed, and marked with grooves, indicating the lines of future division, when the lobes open and disclose the seeds, covered at first with their orange jackets, after the manner of the mace that encloses the nutmeg.

The hardness and toughness of Spindle-wood have long been esteemed in the fashioning of small articles where these qualities are essential, and its common name is a survival of the days when spinning was the occupation of most women. Then spindles were in demand for winding the spun thread upon, and no wood was more suitable for the purpose. Known also as Skewerwood, Prickwood, and Pegwood, all suggestive of uses to which it is or was applied. The young shoots make a very fine charcoal for artists' use.

Among the exotic species cultivated in our parks and gardens are the handsome variegated forms of the Evergreen Spindle (*Euonymus japonicus*) from China and Japan, and the Broad-leaved Spindle (*E. latifolius*) from Europe.

THE PURGING BUCKTHORN

Family RHAMNACEAE   *Rhamnus cathartica*

The Purging Buckthorn may be found in woods, thick hedgerows, and bushy places on commons, southward of Westmorland ; rarely in Ireland.

The yellowish-green leaves are egg-shaped, with toothed edges and short leaf-stalks. Some are gathered into bundles at the ends of the shoots, and many of the branchlets are hardened into spines.

The yellowish-green flowers are very small, and will be found both singly and in clusters from the leaf-axils. There are a four-cleft calyx, four petals, four stamens, or four stigmas, for the sexes are usually on separate plants. The fruit is black, round, and about a quarter of an inch across, containing four stones : ripe in September.

THE ALDER BUCKTHORN

Family RHAMNACEAE   *Frangula alnus*

The Alder Buckthorn is known also as the
Berry-bearing Alder, its leaves, with their lateral
veins, presenting something of the appearance of
the Alder.

Its more slender stems are purplish-brown in
hue, and *all* the leaves are arranged alternatively up

the stems. The leaves differ further from those of the Purging Buckthorn in having plain, untoothed edges, and their veins parallel one to another.

The flowers are similar in size to *R. cath-artica*, but are a paler yellow, fewer in num-ber, and on longer stalks. The parts of the flower, too, are in fives instead of fours ; and the " berry," though similar, is much larger (h a l f - a n-inch diameter) and contains only two seeds. In an unripe con-dition t h e s e fruits yield a good green dye, much used by calico printers and others.

Fruits of Alder Buckthorn.

The wood made into charcoal was said to be the best for the purposes of the gunpowder makers, who knew it by the name of Black Dogwood. The straight shoots of both species of Buckthorn are also used for forming walking and umbrella sticks.

THE HORSE CHESTNUT

Family HIPPOCASTANACEAE   Aesculus hippocastanum

The Horse Chestnut is a native of the mountain regions of Greece, Bulgaria, Iran, and Northern India, and is believed to have been introduced to Britain late in the sixteenth century. It is not a tree that will be found in the woodlands, or even by the wayside ; yet it constantly greets the rambler in the public parks and gardens, where by contrast it exhibits itself as the grandest of all flowering trees. Though the stout, cylindrical bole is short, its erect trunk towers to a height of eighty or a hundred feet, supporting the massive pyramid.

The stout branches take an upward direction at first, then stretch outward and curve downwards, though in winter, when relieved of the weight of foliage, their extremities curl sharply upward, and the great buds, in spring, are almost erect.

These brown buds, with their numerous wraps and liberal coating of resin, afford considerable interest in early spring.

They gradually swell and polish comes upon them through the daily melting of their varnish under the influence of sunshine. Then the outer scales fall flat, the upper parts show green and loose; there is a perceptible lengthening of the shoot, which leaves a space between those outer wraps

and the folded leaves. Next the leaflets separate
and assume a horizontal position as they expand.
The lengthening of the shoot brings the incipient
flower-spike into view.

The leaves are almost circular, but broken up,
finger-fashion, into, usually, seven-toothed leaflets of different sizes, but to prevent overcrowd-
ing their neighbours the portion nearest the leaf-
stalk has taken a wedge-shape. The large size of

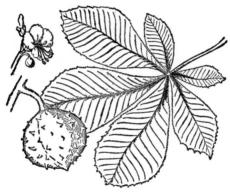

these leaves—as much as eighteen inches across—
leads the non-botanical to regard the leaflets as
being full leaves. On emerging from the bud the
leaves are seen to be covered with down, but as
they expand this is thrown off.

The flowers consist of a bell-shaped calyx with
five lobes, supporting four or five separate petals,
pure white, but splashed and dotted with crimson
and yellow towards the base of the upper ones, to

indicate the way to the nectar glands. There are seven curved stamens, and in their midst a longer curved style proceeding from a roundish ovary with three cells. In each cell there are two seed-eggs, but as a rule only one egg in two of the cells develops into a " nut." The ovary develops into a large fleshy bur, with short stout spines, which splits into three valves when the dark-red glossy seeds are ripe. Though horses will not eat this bitter fruit, cattle, deer, and sheep are fond of it.

The growth of the tree is very rapid, and consequently the timber is soft and of no value where durability is required. Still, its even grain and the ability to take a high polish makes it useful for indoor work, such as cabinet-making, etc.

The tree begins to produce fruit about its twentieth year, and continues to do so nearly every year. Its age is estimated as about two hundred years. The bark, at first smooth, breaks into irregular scales, and in old trees a twist may be developed as shown in the illustration of the bole.

The Red-flowered Horse Chestnut (*Aesculus carnea*) is a smaller and less vigorous tree. It is believed to be a garden hybrid between *A. hippocastanum* and *A. pavia* that made its appearance about 1820.

THE FIELD OR ENGLISH MAPLE

Family ACERACEAE   *Acer campestre*

The Field Maple is thought to be indigenous only from Durham to the southern coast. In Scotland, and probably in Ireland also, it is only an introduced plant that has become naturalized.

It is a small tree that attains a height of twenty to forty feet, but is most familiar as a mere bush.

THE FIELD OR ENGLISH MAPLE

In young trees the pale brown bark is rough and deeply fissured, though with age it becomes smooth.

The leaves range from two to four inches in diameter and are always in pairs exactly opposite to each other. They are kidney-shaped, but cut up into five lobes which are more or less toothed.

Field Maple in fruit

The flowers are greenish-yellow, about a quarter of an inch across, have narrow sepals and petals, eight stamens, and a two-lobed ovary that develops into the pair of broad-winged " keys " about half an inch long, with their bases joined together. Sometimes in late summer these " keys " take on a colouring of deep crimson, afterwards turning brown as they ripen.

THE SYCAMORE

Family ACERACEAE   *Acer pseudoplatanus*

Known also as The Great Maple or False Plane, the Sycamore is not a native tree, but appears to have been introduced from the Continent in the fifteenth century. It is, therefore, well established among us, and by means of its winged seeds distributes itself to remote corners of our islands. It appears to be fond of exposed situations, growing to a large size even near the

sea, where the salt-laden gales would destroy all other deciduous trees.

It grows to a height of sixty or even eighty feet so quickly that it is full-grown when only fifty or sixty years old, though it is supposed to live from 150 to 250 years.

The wood of the Sycamore is firm and fine-grained, and although it can be worked with ease, it is not highly esteemed. The leaves are heart-shaped and cut into five lobes, whose edges are unequally toothed ; they are six or eight inches across. The black patches so frequently seen on Sycamore leaves are the work of a small fungus—*Rhytisma acerinum*.

The flowers are similar to those of the Field

Maple, but larger, and in a long hanging raceme. The "keys" are scimitar-shaped about an inch and a half long, red-brown in colour, produced freely after the tree is about twenty years old.

Like many other Maples, the Sycamore has sap which contains much sugar. Some of this appears also to exude through the leaves.

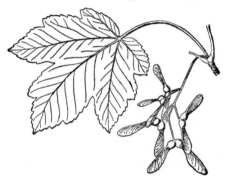

Sycamore in fruit

The Norway Maple (*Acer platanoides*) is a tree of much more recent (1683) introduction from the Continent. Its height is from thirty up to as much as ninety feet, and its early growth is very rapid. The leaves are even larger than those of the Sycamore, of similar shape, but the lobes are only slightly toothed. The clusters of bright yellow flowers appear before the leaves. The tree does not produce seed until it is between forty and fifty years old.

THE LABURNUM

Family PAPILIONACEAE *Laburnum anagyroides*

Although the Laburnums of our parks and gardens have all come from seed, and themselves produce an abundance of it, we do not meet with wayside " escapes " as we might expect to do, having regard to the habit of the tree, and the fact that it is comparatively indifferent respecting character of soil. It has been stated that rabbits are exceedingly fond of the bark, and it may well be that they destroy any young trees that are unprotected.

The tree produces such a glorification of many an ordinary suburban road, when its flowering time comes round, that it would be interesting to

A, Seed-pod.

note its effect as a common object of the hillside and the woodland, against a background furnished by our more sober native trees.

The Laburnum is at home in the mountain forests of Central and Southern Europe, but there is no record of its introduction to Britain. We do know, however, that it has been with us for considerably more than three hundred years, as it was referred to in a publication of 1597.

It belongs to the great Pea and Bean family (*Papilionaceae*), and is very closely related to the Common Broom, whose solitary flowers those of the Laburnum's drooping racemes nearly resemble.

Ordinarily it is only a low tree about twenty feet in height, but in favourable situations it may attain to thirty feet or more. Some of the larger Laburnums, however, are of a distinct species (*L. alpinum*).

The pale round branches are clothed with leaves that are divided into three oval lance-shaped leaflets, covered on the underside with silvery down. Both leaves and golden flowers appear simultaneously in May, but from the fact that the flowers are gathered into numerous long pendulous racemes, their blaze of colour makes the leaves almost invisible.

The flowers are succeeded by long downy pods, like those of the Bean and Pea, containing many seeds, which are of a dangerously violent emetic character when introduced to the human stomach.

The dark wood is of a coarse grain ; but, in spite of this, hard and enduring, and taking a good polish. It is chiefly used by musical instrument makers, wood turners, and cabinet-makers.

Common local names are Golden Chain, suggested by the strings of flowers, and Bean-trefoil and Pea-tree, having reference to the leaves and seed-pods respectively.

THE LOCUST TREE

Family PAPILIONACEAE   *Robinia pseudacacia*

Although the Locust, known also as False
Acacia, is little planted now, it is only paying the
penalty for having had its merits enormously
exaggerated. William Cobbett, on his return
from the United States of America about 1820,

preached salvation to the timber grower through the planting of *Robinia*. So great was the demand thus created that Cobbett himself started a nursery

for the propagation and supply of the trees, which could not be produced fast enough to meet the demand. It was thought to be an entirely new introduction, though it had been grown in this country as an ornamental tree for nearly two hundred years!

Its wood is hard, strong, and durable, but liable to crack, and of limited utility.

The Locust is a tree of light and graceful proportions, its branches being long and slender. The leaves are long and narrow, broken up into a large number of small oval leaflets. The stipules which are found at the base of the leaf-stalk in many plants, are in this genus converted into sharp spines.

The flowers, of similar pea-shape to those of the Laburnum, are white and fragrant. They are in long loose racemes, which droop from the axils of the leaves in May. The seed-pods are very thin, and of a dark brown hue.

This was one of the first American trees to be brought to Europe early in the seventeenth century, and the name of Locust came with it.

Seed-pod on left

It was then thought to be identical with the African Acacia. Linnaeus named the genus in honour of Jean Robin, a French botanist, whose son, an official at the Jardin des Plantes, was the first to cultivate the tree in Europe. The American missionaries believed it was the tree upon whose fruit, with the addition of wild honey, John the Baptist survived in the wilderness.

It is also known as Silver Chain and as White Laburnum.

THE SLOE OR BLACKTHORN

Family ROSACEAE   *Prunus spinosa*

The Sloe is the rigid many-branched shrub, with stiletto-like tips, that flourishes on some of our commons and in our hedgerows.

The blackish bark that gives its name to the shrub sets off to advantage, in March or April, the pure white starry blossoms that brave the cold blasts before the leaf-buds dare unfurl their coverings.

The branches and twigs turn in every direction, so that it is impossible to thrust one's hand into a Blackthorn bush without getting considerably scratched. The well-known flower consists of a

five-lobed calyx, five white petals, and from fifteen to twenty stamens round the single carpel. The stigma matures in advance of the stamens, so that it has usually been fertilized by bee-borne pollen from another Sloe before its own anthers have disclosed their pollen.

The fruit is about half an inch across, globose in form, and held erect upon its short stalk; black, but its blackness hidden by a delicate " bloom " which gives it a purplish hue.

THE BULLACE

Family ROSACEAE   *Prunus insititia*

The Bullace differs from the Sloe in having *brown* bark, the branches *straight* and only a few of them ending in spines, the leaves larger, broader, more coarsely toothed, and downy on the underside. The flowers, too, have broader petals, and the fruit—which may be black or yellow—droops, and is about three-quarters of an inch in diameter.

In many places where the Bullace grows it can only be regarded as an escape from cultivation.

THE WILD PLUM

Family ROSACEAE   *Prunus domestica*

This species has also brown bark, its branches straight, and not ending in spines. The downiness noticed on the underside of the Bullace leaves is here restricted to the ribs of the leaf.

The fruit attains a diameter of an inch or an inch and a half.

Although found occasionally in hedgerows, this species is not indigenous in any part of our islands. Probably the only country in which it is really indigenous is Western Asia ; but its numerous cultivated forms are widely distributed.

THE GEAN

Family ROSACEAE   *Prunus avium*

There are three native Wild Cherries in the British Islands, viz.: The Gean (*P. avium*), the Wild or Dwarf Cherry (*P. cerasus*), and the Bird Cherry (*P. padus*). Of these the Gean is the species most widely distributed throughout our country.

THE GEAN

The Gean attains a height of eighty to a hundred feet, with short, stout branches that take an upward direction. The leaves are large, broadly oval, with toothed edges, and downy on the underside. They always droop from the branches, and in spring they are of a bronzy-brown tint,

afterwards changing to pale green. Soon after the leaves have unfolded they are almost hidden by the umbels of white flowers, which have five heart-shaped petals, and whose anthers and stigmas mature simultaneously.

The firm-fleshed fruit is heart-shaped, black or red, with scanty juice which stains the fingers.

This is believed to be the original wild stock from which our Black Hearts and Bigarreau Cherries have been evolved by the cultivator.

THE WILD OR DWARF CHERRY

Family ROSACEAE   *Prunus cerasus*

The Wild or Dwarf Cherry is bush-like, for it sends up suckers around the main stem. The branches are slender and drooping. The leaves are smooth and deep blue-green, with round-toothed edges. The flowers are not so open as in

the Gean, but retain more of the cup-shape, whilst the notched petals are oval and firmer.

The fruit is round, with red skin and juicy flesh of a distinctly acid character. The Morello, The May Duke, and the Kentish Cherries are considered to be derived from this species.

P. cerasus does not extend farther north than Cumberland. In Ireland it is found in hedgerows.

THE BIRD CHERRY

Family ROSACEAE   *Prunus padus*

The Bird Cherry forms a tree from ten to thirty feet in height, with elliptic-shaped leaves, which have their edges doubly cut into fine teeth.

The flowers are not clustered in umbels, as in the Gean and the Wild Cherry, but in a loose

THE BIRD CHERRY

raceme springing from lateral spurs of new growth. The flowers are erect when they open, and the stigmas mature before the anthers, so that cross-fertilization is favoured in this species. After fertilization the flower droops, to be out of the way of the bees in their visits to the unfertilized blossoms. The petals in this species look as if their edges had been gnawed.

The fruits are small, black, and very bitter to the taste, with a wrinkled stone.

This is a northern species, coming not further south than Leicestershire and South Wales.

The Gean, the Wild Cherry, and the Bird Cherry all flower in late April or early May.

Cherry wood is strong, fine-grained, and of a red colour. It is easily worked, and susceptible of a high polish.

59

THE WILD PEAR

Family ROSACEAE   *Pyrus communis*

The Wild Pear is regarded as more probably a species originally introduced by man, and has maintained its hold upon the new land. Upon this assumption it is probable that the introduced specimens were already somewhat cultivated, but when they became wild they reverted to the original condition of the species.

It is a small tree, from twenty to sixty feet in height, of somewhat pyramidal form. The twigs, which are usually of a drooping tendency, are also much given to ending in spines.

The leaves are toothed, oval in shape, with blunt-toothed edges, and downy on the lower surface. Along the new shoots they are arranged alternately on opposite sides, but on shoots a year old they are produced in clusters.

The flowers, about an inch across, are white and clustered in corymbs of five to twelve. They appear in April and May, and are of the Wild Rose type. There are numerous stamens, three to five styles, which ripen before the stamens, five petals, and the calyx with a five-lobed mouth, representing the five sepals.

When the flower opens it is ready for fertilization, but as the stamens of that flower are not yet mature this can only be accomplished by pollen brought by the bees from other flowers. The effect of pollination is to cause special vegetative activity in the neighbourhood of the ovary, resulting in the thickening of the flesh of the calyx-tube

around it, until it has become the characteristic pear-shape, an inch or two in length.

The fruit is green until about November, when it turns yellow. It is too harsh a character to be fit for eating.

The Pear is a long-lived tree, growing singly or in small groups on dry plains. It attains a height of about fifty feet in thirty years, and its girth may then be three or four feet. The timber is fine-grained, strong, and heavy, with a reddish tinge.

THE WILD APPLE OR CRAB

Family ROSACEAE   *Malus sylvestris*

The Apple appears to have been the subject of cultural attention from very early times. This is proved from the similarity of the equivalents for our word Apple in all the Celtic and Sclavonian languages, showing by their common origin that the fruit was of sufficient importance to have a distinctive name long before the separation of the peoples of Northern Europe.

The Wild Apple is rounded in general form and the branches spread widely when young, and droop somewhat when older. As a tree it varies in height from twenty to fifty feet, though many examples of good age still retain the dimensions of a bush. The bole is usually more or less crooked like the older branches. The brown bark is not very rough, though its numerous fissures and cracks give it a rugged appearance.

THE WILD APPLE OR CRAB

Its wood, like that of the Pear, is hard and fine-grained, but instead of having a reddish tinge, there is a tendency to brownish.

The leaves vary in shape, but are more or less oblong, smooth above, sometimes downy on the lower surface when young, and with toothed edges.

The flowers are about the same size as those of the Wild Pear, but their white petals are beautifully tinted and streaked with pink. They are clustered together with the foot-stalks of similar length, starting from a common base.

The fruit is almost spherical, and instead of the foot-stalk gradually merging into the apple, the attachment is always in a depression of the latter.

In the typical form of the Wild Apple the yellow and red fruits hang by their slender stalks, and they are about an inch across, and so rich in malic acid as to be unfit for food in their natural state.

The Wild Apple is found all over the United Kingdom as far north as the Clyde, and wherever

it is known to occur it is worth a special visit in May, when all its branches and shoots are rendered beautiful by the abundance of delicately tinted and fragrant flowers. It is attractive also in the autumn, when the miniature apples hang from the boughs.

THE WHITEBEAM

Family ROSACEAE   *Sorbus aria*

Owing to its very local occurrence, the White-beam, though widely distributed, is one of the less known of our trees and shrubs. It comes into both these categories according to the situation of its growth, for whilst in exposed mountainous localities a specimen of mature age may be no more than four or five feet high, and of bush-like growth, under the lee of a wood, and on calcareous soil, it will be an erect and graceful tree of pyramidal form, whose apex is forty feet from the ground.

In its early years growth is tolerably rapid, but at the age of ten it slackens pace, and after attaining its majority its progress is very slow. The bark is smooth and little subject to cracks and fissures. The branches, except a few of the lowest, all have an upward tendency. Its wood is fine-grained, very hard, white, but inclined to yellow.

In the typical form the leaves are a broad oval in shape, with the edges coarsely toothed or cut into lobes, the upper side smooth, and the lower side clothed with white cottony down, the almost straight nerves strongly marked.

The white flowers, which appear in May or

June, are only half an inch across, and gathered into loose clusters. They are succeeded by nearly round scarlet fruits, half an inch in diameter, known in Lancashire and Westmorland as Chess-apples. These are very sharp and rough to the taste, but when kept like Medlars, till they begin to decay, are far from unpleasant.

This form is only found from the Midlands to the South of England as far west as Devon, and in Ireland.

There are several closely allied species differing mainly in the leaves. *Sorbus latifolia*, also known as *Pyrus latifolia*, has broader leaves, divided into wedge-shaped lobes, the cottony down beneath being grey and the nerves less prominent. This species is rare in hilly woods. *Sorbus intermedia*, also known as *Pyrus scandica*, has the leaves more deeply divided into rounded or oblong lobes. It is usually found as a cultivated tree.

Other names for the Whitebeam include Hen-apple, Cumberland Hawthorn, Hoar Withy and Whipcrop.

It should be noted that *S. aria* must not be called the Whitebeam *tree*, for the word *beam* is the Saxon equivalent for tree.

THE WILD SERVICE TREE

Family ROSACEAE   *Sorbus torminalis*

This species is a small tree of local occurrence, which does not extend farther north than Lancashire. In general appearance it may be taken for the Whitebeam, but closer inspection will reveal the following differences. The leaves, which are cut into tapering lobes and coarsely toothed, are heart-shaped at the base; when young they are slightly downy beneath, but when mature they are smooth on both sides.

The flowers are similar in size and colour to those of the Whitebeam, but the fruit is smaller, less globular, and the colour is greenish-brown. The flowers appear in April and May, and the fruit, which is of a very dry, juiceless character, is ripe in November. In some localities these fruits are marketed, but they require to be kept like Medlars, until decay sets in, before they are fit to be eaten. This tree should not be confused with the True Service Tree (*Sorbus domestica*), details of which are given on page 74.

THE MOUNTAIN ASH OR ROWAN

Family ROSACEAE   *Sorbus aucuparia*

In recent years the Mountain Ash has come so much into favour that it is now one of the commonest of the trees planted in suburban gardens and fore-courts. Its hardiness, its indifference to the character of the soil, the fact that other plants will grow beneath it, and the absence of need for pruning, make it most suitable and popular for growth in restricted areas. But the wood on the hillside is the natural home of the Mountain Ash, and in the Highlands of Scotland its vertical range extends to 2,600 feet above sea-level.

The Mountain Ash attains a height of from thirty to fifty feet, and has a straight, clean bole, clothed in smooth grey bark, scarred horizontally as though it had been scored with a knife. All the branches have an upward tendency, and the shoots bear the long feathery leaves, whose division into eleven to fifteen slender leaflets suggests *the* Ash. It is not even remotely allied to *Fraxinus excelsior*, and the similarity of leaf-division is the only point of resemblance between them.

These leaflets have toothed edges, are paler on the underside, and in a young condition the midrib and nerves are hairy.

THE MOUNTAIN ASH OR ROWAN

The creamy-white flowers are like little Hawthorn blossoms, though only half the size, and they appear in dense clusters in May or June.

The fruits are miniature apples, of the size of holly berries, bright scarlet without and yellow within. They ripen in September, and are then

a great attraction to thrushes, blackbirds, and their kind, who rapidly strip the tree of them. At first sight this may appear like frustrating the tree's object in producing fruit, but the attractive flesh is a mere bait to induce the birds to pass the seeds through their intestines, and thus get them sown far and wide. By this method the process of germination is considerably hastened, whereas by hand-sowing the seeds lie in the earth for eighteen months before shooting.

All the species of *Sorbus* produce their fruits with this object, the larger more or less brownish ones being attractive to mammals, the smaller and red-coloured ones to birds. The seeds have leathery jackets to protect them from the action of the digestive fluids, and are further wrapped in a parchmenty, bony, or wooden " core," with a similar object. In the case of the Mountain Ash this is very like wood.

In the South of Britain the Mountain Ash is chiefly grown as underwood and used as a nurse for oaks and other timber trees, which soon out-grow and kill it ; so that in the woods it is seldom allowed to grow into a fully developed tree, but, thanks to the birds, it comes up on the common and the hillside, and has a chance of producing its masses of ruby fruit.

Its wood is tough and elastic, but, owing to the smallness of its girth, it does not produce timber of any size.

Among the numerous names of the Mountain Ash are Quickbeam, White Ash (from the colour of the flowers), Witch-wood, and Witchen. Quickbeam is in allusion to the constant move-ment of the foliage, quick being the Anglo-Saxon *cwic*, alive. Witch-wood and Witchen are also forms of *cwic*.

THE TRUE SERVICE TREE

Family ROSACEAE   *Sorbus domestica*

The True Service closely resembles the Mountain Ash in habit and foliage, but it is not a native of Britain, though it used to be claimed as such. It is occasionally cultivated here, and a brief account of its points of difference from the Mountain Ash is now given.

A comparison of the boles of the two species will show a great difference ; that of the Mountain Ash being smooth, whilst that of the Service is rugged.

The leaf is similarly broken up into paired leaflets, but these are broader, and are downy on b o t h u p p e r and lower sides. The white flowers are as large as May-blossoms, and the fruits are greenish-brown, about four times the size of Rowan-berries. In winter, w h e n there are n e i t h e r leaves, flowers, nor fruits to help in the distinction, the bark may be taken in conjunction with the leaf-buds, which are green, smooth and viscid in this species, whilst those of the Mountain Ash are black and downy.

The wood is described as the hardest and heaviest of all the trees indigenous to Europe.

THE MEDLAR

Family ROSACEAE   *Mespilus germanica*

The Medlar is a small tree, native of Iran, Asia Minor, and Greece, but which is generally held to occur in England and the Channel Islands only as an escape from cultivation. The theory is that the tree was introduced at some date prior

to 1596—when we have record of its being in cultivation here—and that the Medlar trees growing in the hedges of south and middle England are from seeds of these cultivated trees, which have been sown by birds, or more probably mammals who have eaten the fruit. The fact that it is not found in woods is taken as evidence that it is non-indigenous. Such evidence is not the most convincing, but it is the best available.

It should be noted, however, that the agents credited with its distribution along our hedgerows have free access to the woods, and that if these places were favourable to the growth of the Medlar, we should probably find it there, whether indigenous or not. Much more conclusive is its restricted distribution abroad, as already indicated. One would not expect to find a tree whose nearest home is Greece, leaping over the whole of Europe and appearing as a native of Britain.

In its wild condition the Medlar is a much-branched and spiny tree, from ten to twenty feet high, in these respects resembling the Hawthorn; but, like the Pear, it puts off its defences when cultivated.

Its leaves are large and undivided, of an oblong-lance shape, downy beneath, and sometimes with the edges very finely toothed.

The solitary white or pale pink flowers are about one and a half inches across, with a woolly calyx, whose five tips expand into leafy growths. They appear in May or June, and are succeeded by brown fruits, about an inch across, which may be described as round, with a depressed top, which is ornamented with the remains of the calyx-lobes. They ripen in October or November.

THE HAWTHORN

Family ROSACEAE   *Crataegus monogyna*

Though distributed as a wild tree throughout
the length and breadth of the British Isles, we
are all more familiar with the Hawthorn as planted
material in the construction of hedges, and this is
a use to which it has been put ever since land was
plotted out and enclosed.

THE HAWTHORN

Where the Hawthorn is allowed its natural growth, it attains a height of forty feet, with a circumference between three and ten feet. On our

commons, where in their youth the Hawthorns have to submit to much mutilation from browsing animals, their growth is spoiled; but though some of these never become more than bushes tangled up with Blackthorn into small thickets, there are others that form a distinct bole and a round head of branches from ten to twenty feet high, which in late May or early June look like solid masses of snow.

The well-known lobed leaves are very variable in both size and shape, and the degree to which they are cut. They are a favourite food with horses and oxen, who would demolish the hedges that confine them to the fields but for the spines which protect at least the older branches.

The white flowers are about three-quarters of
an inch across, borne in numerous corymbs. The
pink anthers give relief to the uniform whiteness
of the petals. The flowers, though usually sweet-
scented, occasionally give forth a very unpleasant
odour.

The familiar fruits, too, instead of their usual
crimson, are yellow occasionally, as in the Holly.
In favourable years these are so plentiful that they
quite kill the effect of the dark-green leaves, and
when such a tree is seen in the October sunshine,
it appears to be glowing with fire. Beneath the
ripe, mealy flesh, there is a hard, bony core, in
whose cells the seeds are protected from digestion
when the fruit has been swallowed by a bird.

The Hawthorn is said to live from a hundred to
three hundred years. Its wood is both hard and
tough.

THE DOGWOOD OR CORNEL

Family CORNACEAE   *Cornus sanguinea*

Among the hedgerow and copse, the Dogwood or Cornel is apt to be overlooked as Privet,
to which it bears a resemblance by its opposite
leaves and clusters of small white flowers. It is
widely distributed over Britain as far north as
Westmorland. It does not occur in Scotland,

and is rare in Ireland. It grows to a height of six or eight feet, and is clothed with opposite oval leaves, which are smooth on both surfaces.

The flowers secrete nectar and are produced in June or July at the extremities of the branches in dense round cymes. They are small, opaque white, with four petals and four stamens; the central flower which opens first, has five petals and

stamens. Their unpleasant odour appears to attract flies and small beetles.

The flowers are succeeded by small green berries, which turn purple-black about September, and are exceedingly bitter. They are said to yield an oil which is used in France for soap-making, and has been here burned in lamps.

The Dogwood has a great variety of local names. Dogwood or Dagwood was the wood of which dags, goads, and skewers were made, because, as the Latin *Cornus* signifies, it was of horny hardness and toughness.

THE ELDER

The Elder is more a tree of the wayside than of the woodland, often of low bushy growth ; but where it finds good loamy soil with abundant moisture it will attain a height of twenty feet.

None of our trees grows more rapidly in its

earliest years, and any bit of its living wood will readily take root, so that its presence in the hedge is often due to planting for the purpose of rapidly erecting a live screen. Its quickly grown juicy shoots soon harden into a tube of tough wood with a core of pith which is readily extracted, and

renders the tube available as a blow-pipe, a pop-gun, or a music pipe. Such uses have been known from remote antiquity. It is thus probable that the housewife got her bellows, the musician his pipe, and the small boy his pop-gun, all from the same source.

The stems are coated with a grey corky bark. When old, the wood becomes hard and heavy, and has been used as a substitute for box.

The leaf is divided into five, seven, or nine oval leaflets with toothed edges.

The flower is *rotate* in form, that is, the corolla

forms a very short tube, from the mouth of which five petal-like lobes spread flat. This is a quarter of an inch broad, and creamy-white in colour, giving out an odour which some persons consider offensive. Large numbers of these small flowers are gathered into flat-topped cymes, five or six inches in diameter. The primary stalks of these cymes are five in number.

The flowers are succeeded by small globular berries, ultimately of a purple-black hue, and of mawkish flavour, which are yet much sought after by country people for the making of Elderberry Wine, which they credit with marvellous medicinal powers. It is doubtful if the Elder still retains among rustic folk much of the reputation of long ago for the medicinal properties of its leaves, bark, and berries.

Occasionally one may find in the hedgerow an Elder with its leaflets deeply cut into very slender lobes, so that the leaf has resemblance to that of Fool's Parsley. This is an escape from cultivation—a garden variety (*laciniata*) known as the Cut-leaved or Parsley-leaved Elder and decidedly ornamental.

THE GUELDER ROSE

Family CAPRIFOLIACEAE   *Viburnum opulus*

The distribution of the Guelder Rose as a wild plant extends northwards to Caithness, although it is generally rare in Scotland. It occurs throughout Ireland.

The Guelder Rose is very closely related to the Wayfaring-tree, but the differences between them

are so great that there is little danger of the observer confusing them. The Guelder Rose does not grow so tall as its congener, twelve feet being about the extreme height in its wild state, and often it is several feet less.

It is not so fond of dry soils, and is more frequently found in the copse, where it is not subject to the extremes of heat and cold that have produced the hairy covering of the Wayfaring-tree.

The stems and branches are quite smooth, and the leaf-buds are wrapped in scales. The young leaves, it is true, are covered with down when they break from the bud, but they throw this off as they expand to their full size.

The leaf is divided into three deeply toothed lobes. The flower-head is rounded and in the mass about the same size as those of the Wayfaring-tree. The outer row of flowers are about three times the size of the others—but they are entirely without stamens or pistil! The inner and perfect flowers are creamy-white, bell-shaped, and they secrete nectar. Both stamens and stigma mature simultaneously.

The fruits are almost round, and of a clear, translucent red. Respecting these fruits it is recorded that for any one who enjoys the sight of red berries in the most jewel-like splendour, there is nothing in winter like *V. opulus*, and if the rambler meets with a fine specimen just as it is caught by the level rays of a crimson sunset, he will behold a shrub whose fruits appear as jewels. These juicy fruits, though so pleasing to the sight, are nauseous to the taste although in Scandinavia they are sometimes eaten with a mixture of honey and flour.

In the Cotswolds the Guelder Rose is known as King's Crown, from the " King of the May " having been crowned with a chaplet of it. Another name for it is Water Elder, presumably given on account of the similar appearance of the flower-clusters in Guelder Rose and Elder.

Family CAPRIFOLIACEAE   *Viburnum lantana*

    The Wayfaring-tree may be looked for wherever the soil is dry, as far north as Yorkshire. Though not confined to chalk-hills it finds such conditions best and is there especially abundant. It is not indigenous in either Scotland or Ireland.

THE WAYFARING-TREE

Though it grows to a height of twenty feet in places, it can never properly be called a tree. Its downy stems are never very stout. They branch a good deal, and are always given off in pairs, a branch from each side of the stem at exactly the same height; the leaves are produced in the same

order. These leaves, which are three or four inches in length, are much wrinkled, heart-shaped, with a blunt, small end, white beneath, and the edges very finely toothed.

The flower-cluster is a cyme, and it should be noted that all the white flowers comprised in it are of the same size and form, the corollas being funnel-shaped, with five lobes, and the five stamens are extruded from the mouth. The flowers, which are jointed to the stalks, are out in May and June, and the flattened oval fruits that follow are at first red and then black.

THE WAYFARING-TREE

The Wayfaring-tree is a bold plant; in winter showing its large naked buds, all rough with starry hairs, which keep off frost, as well as do the many scales and thick varnish of Horse Chestnut buds. In summer the broad, hairy leaves look as dusty as a miller's coat, and above them spread the slightly rounded heads of white flowers; later, the flowers are succeeded by bunches of glowing coral beads, that in autumn become beads of jet.

The local names of this shrub include Mealy-tree, Whipcrop, Cotton-tree, Cottoner, Coventree, Lithe-wort, Lithy-tree, Twist-wood, White-wood. Mealy-tree, Cotton tree, Cottoner, and White-wood all have obvious reference to the appearance of the young shoots and leaves, due to the presence of the white hairs with which they are covered. Lithe-wort and Lithy-tree, also Twist-wood and Whipcrop, indicate the supple and elastic character of the branches, which are often used instead of Withy to bind up a bundle of sticks or vegetables, or to make a loop for a gate fastener. On the Continent the shoots, when only a year old, are used in basket-weaving, and, when a year or two older, serve for pipe-stems.

THE STRAWBERRY-TREE

Family ERICACEAE   *Arbutus unedo*

Though the Strawberry-tree may be seen in parks and gardens, it will not be found in the woods or by the waysides in Great Britain; but in parts of Ireland it is native. Killarney, Muck-ross, and Bantry are stated as its Irish stations, but it has also been found in the woods at Woodstock, Co. Kilkenny, in a situation where it seemed unlikely such a tree would be planted.

In Ireland it attains a maximum height of forty feet, though in England it rarely exceeds twenty or thirty feet under cultivation.

The bark is rough and scaly, tinged with red, and twisted.

The leathery leaves are more or less oval, two or three inches long, with toothed edges and hairy stalks. Although arranged alternately on the shoots, they present the appearance at a little distance of being clustered, rosette fashion, at the tips of the twigs.

THE STRAWBERRY-TREE

The creamy-white or pinkish flowers are clustered in drooping racemes at the ends of the twigs, and are about one-third of an inch across, bell-shaped. After the fertilization of the seeds the corollas drop off, so that in the flowering season (September and October) the ground beneath will usually be found strewn with them.

The fruit is a round berry, of an orange-red hue, whose surface is completely studded with little points. As these berries do not come to maturity until about fourteen months after the flowers have dropped their corollas, both flowers and almost full-formed fruit may be seen on the tree at the same time. They are not eatable until quite ripe, and even then they are too austere to suit everybody's taste. In truth, we have it on the testimony of Pliny that the old Latin name *Unedo*, now included in the specific scientific name, was given to it because to eat one of these tree strawberries was a sufficiently extensive acquaintance for most persons.

It is perhaps unnecessary to add that, in spite of the name, there is no relationship existing between this tree and *the* Strawberry; nor is there more than a faint superficial resemblance between the fruits of the two plants. The Strawberry belongs to the great Rose family, whilst the nearest British connections of the *Arbutus* are the Bilberries and Heaths.

Family OLEACEAE   *Fraxinus excelsior*

So commanding, yet at the same time so light and graceful, does a well-grown Ash appear, that it has been called the " Venus of the Woods." This may appear to be rather too close an approach to the " Lady of the Woods " (Birch), but it well expresses the characteristics of the two. They

are both exceedingly graceful, but the beauty of
the Birch is that of the nymph, whilst that of the
Ash is the combined grace and strength of the
goddess.

It is in a meadow,
or on the outskirts
of a wood, or in the
hedgerow, where it
is not hemmed in
by other trees, and
where both soil and
atmosphere are
moist and cool;
where it has had
elbow-room to reach
its long, graceful
arms upwards and
outwards, and to
cover them with the
plumy circlets of
long leaves, that the
Ash is able to do
credit to the name
bestowed upon it.

Before the reign
of iron and steel was
so universal, Ash
timber was in de-
mand for many uses

where the metals have now supplanted it.

It was then grown as a hedgerow tree far more
widely than is now the case. No doubt the
noxious drip and shade of the Ash have had much
to do with this abandonment of it, for few things
can live beneath it—a condition which quickly

exhausts and drains the soil, and so starves out other plants. Although it thus drains the surface soil, it is not dependent upon these upper layers for food, for its much-branched roots extend very deeply in the porous soils it prefers.

The Ash has a preference for the northern and eastern sides of hills, where the atmosphere is moist and cool, and the soil deep and porous, for it loves free and not stagnant moisture for its roots. A well-grown Ash attains a height of eighty to one hundred feet.

The bark of both trunk and branches is pale grey, and it is supposed that this is the origin of the tree's English name. On examining the leafless branches in early spring, two things will strike the observer—the blackness of the big opposite leaf-buds, and the stoutness of the twigs. This latter fact is due to the great size of the leaves they will have to support, which implies a considerable strain in wind or rain.

What are generally regarded as the leaves of the Ash are only leaflets, though they are equal in size to the leaves of most of our trees. The largest of the leaflets is about three inches in length, and there are from four to seven—mostly six—pairs, and an odd terminal one, to each leaf. They are lance-shaped with toothed edges. They appear rather late and are amongst the earliest to depart.

The flowers of the Ash are very poor affairs, for they have neither calyx nor corolla, though their association in large clusters makes them fairly conspicuous as they droop from the sides of the branches in April or May. Stamens and pistils are borne by the same or separate flowers, and both kinds or one only may be found on the same tree. The pistil is a greenish-yellow pear-shaped body, and the stamens are very dark purple.

The flowers are succeeded by bunches of " keys "—each one, when ripe, a narrow-oblong

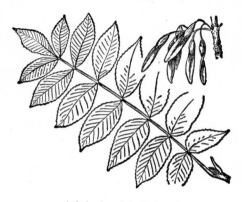

Ash leaf and fruit (keys)

scale, with a notch at one end and a seed lying within at the other. The correct name of these " keys " is samaras. Examining a bunch of these " keys " one is struck by the fact that they all have a little twist in the wing, which causes the " key " to spin steadily on the wind and reach the earth seed-end first. They are, therefore, sometimes known as " spinners." These are ripe in October; but though the trees produce seed nearly every year after the fortieth, the observer may chance to look at a dozen Ashes before one is discovered that bears a seed. The reason for this is the fact that some trees have no female blossoms. The seeds do not germinate until the second spring after they are sown.

The Ash is not one of the long-lived trees, its natural span being about two hundred years, but its wood is regarded as best between the ages of thirty and sixty years. So strong and elastic is the Ash timber when taken from young trees, that it is claimed it will bear a greater strain than any other European timber of equal thickness. Much of the Ash-wood obtained from Ash-coppice, where only small diameters are needed, is used for the fashioning of oars, axe and hammer shafts, and similar purposes.

Useful also in many agricultural operations. Cattle and horses are fond of Ash leaves, which were formerly much used for fodder, but it is said that to indulge cows in this food is fatal to the production of good butter from their milk.

THE BAY TREE

Family LAURACEAE   *Laurus nobilis*

The Bay is the true Laurel, of whose leaves and berries the wreaths were made in ancient days for poets and conquerors.

Naturally it is more of a shrub than a tree, for though it often attains a height of sixty feet, it persists in sending up so many suckers that the tree-like character is sometimes lost.

The Bay is a native of Southern Europe, whence it was introduced at some date prior to 1562.

The evergreen leaves are lance-shaped, without toothed edges, and arranged alternately on the branchlets.

Not all the trees produce the berries, for the sexes are in distinct individuals, and all the white or yellowish four-parted flowers on one tree are stamen-bearing, whilst on another individual they all bear ovaries and no stamens.

The flowers will be found in April or May.

The berries, at first green, ultimately become of a dark purple hue, and are ripe in October.

The Bay is grown chiefly as a shrubbery ornament, and can only survive our winters out-of-doors in the South of England.

THE BOX

Family BUXACEAE   *Buxus sempervirens*

Though frequently met with in parks and ornamental grounds, there are only a few places in this
country where the Box is apparently indigenous.
These are in the counties of Surrey, Kent, Buck-
ingham, and Gloucester. On the famous Box
Hill, near Dorking, in Surrey, it may be seen

attaining its proper proportions as a small tree, and in sufficient abundance to form groves covering a considerable area. Box-hill is in no sense a

plantation; its slopes and summit are clothed with a natural mixed wood of Box, Oak, Beech, and Yew.

The Box grows to a height of twenty or thirty feet with a girth of about three feet. Its slender branches are clothed with small, oblong, l e a t h e r y leaves, about an inch in length, polished on the upper side, e v e r g r e e n, and opposite.

The flowers may be looked for from January to May, and will be found clustered between the leaf and the stem. They are quite small and inconspicuous, of a whitish-green colour, and the sexes are in separate flowers. The uppermost one in the centre of each cluster is a female flower; the others are males. The males consist of four sepals, enclosing a rudimentary ovary, from beneath which spring four stamens. The sepals of the female flower vary in number, from four to twelve, and enclose a rounded ovary with three styles, which are ripe and protruded before the males open. This develops into the three-celled capsule with three diverging beaks, which correspond with the styles, and in each cell there are one or two black seeds.

A. Male flowers; B. Female flowers.

The growth of the tree is very slow, and, in consequence, the grain of the wood is very fine. It is also very hard, and so heavy that, alone among our native woods, it will not float in water.

On account of its fine grain and hardness, it is in request by the wood-turner and mathematical instrument maker, and was formerly largely prepared for use by the wood-engraver for " wood-cuts."

Family ULMACEAE *Ulmus*

Wych Elm.

There are four species of Elm commonly met with in England. The Wych Elm (*Ulmus glabra*), the Smooth-leaved Elm (*U. carpinifolia*), the Plot's Elm (*U. plotii*), and the English Elm (*U. procera*). In addition there is the Cornish

Elm (*Ulmus stricta*) confined to Devon and Cornwall, and hybrids such as the Dutch Elm (*Ulmus hollandica*), and the Huntingdon Elm (*Ulmus vegeta*).

It had been accepted generally that the English Elm had been introduced by the Romans; but it proves to be unknown as a wild tree except in England.

The Wych Elm is also known as Mountain Elm, Scots Elm, and Witch Hazel, under the Latin name *montana*.

Although the Wych Elm| is found at an elevation of 1,300 feet in Yorkshire, and the English Elm at 1,500 feet in

Bole of Wych Elm.

Derbyshire, they are distinctly trees of the lowlands and valleys.

The Wych Elm forms a trunk of large size, from eighty to one hundred and twenty feet or more in height, with a girth of fifty feet, and covered with rough bark. Its long slender branches spread widely with a downward tendency, the downy forking twigs bearing their leaves in a straight row along each side.

The leaves are somewhat oval in general form,

Wych-Elm with fruits

but the two sides of the midrib are unequal in size and shape. Their edges are toothed, and the surfaces are rough and harsh to the touch. The hairs that cover the strong ribs on the under surface serve to protect the breathing pores from the dust. On leaves of the pendulous form of this tree when grown in city parks and gardens these hairs will often be found to be quite black with the soot particles gathered from the air. Trees need carbon, but in a gross form they are often suffocated by it.

The dark red flowers are produced in bunches,

in February or March, from the sides of the branches. They are a quarter of an inch long, bell-shaped, their edges cut into lobes, and finely fringed. The ovary, with its two styles, is surrounded by four or five stamens with purple anthers. They appear before the leaf-buds have opened, and are dependent on the wind for the transfer of pollen.

The fruit is an oblong *samara*, about an inch long. This consists of a single seed in the centre, invested by a thin envelope, which forms a light membranous wing, which gives it buoyancy and enables it to float through the air to a little distance. These seeds are not produced until about the thirtieth year of the tree's life, and although they are ripened almost annually thereafter, good crops are biennial or triennial only.

The Wych Elm never or very rarely produces suckers.

THE ENGLISH ELM

Family ULMACEAE   *Ulmus procera*

The Elm most frequently seen is the English Elm, which is therefore entitled to its alternative name of Common Elm. Constantly grown as a hedgerow tree, it is met with at every turn, though it is much less plentiful in Scotland than in other parts of the United Kingdom.

THE ENGLISH ELM

It is in all respects very similar to the Wych Elm, but its leaves are smaller—usually from two to three inches long, the twigs often covered with a corky bark, and the leaves do not have the base overlapping the leaf-stalk as in *U. glabra*.

The leaves are proportionately narrower than those of the Wych Elm, and it will be found that the hairs which cover the midrib below possess in minor degree the irritating qualities of the Nettle's stings. This is a fact not generally known. Examination of these hairs shows that they are constructed much on the same plan as those of the Nettle—a member of a closely related family, by the way.

The fact that these leaves are browsed by cattle and deer may explain this development of the hairs, which, whilst they may serve to keep off sheep, have not yet reached a degree of acridity sufficient to protect them from the larger beasts.

Both flowers and samaras are about a third smaller than those of the Wych Elm ; but fertile seed is very seldom produced, and the tree seeks to reproduce itself by throwing up abundant suckers round the base of the bole, and even from root-branches at a considerable distance from the

English Elm with fruits

trunk. These, of course, if allowed to grow, would soon surround the tree with copse.

The English Elm often attains a greater height with its straighter trunk than the Wych Elm, but its girth is not so great, seldom being more than twenty feet. Its dark wood is harder and finer grained than that produced by the Wych Elm. Its favour as a hedgerow tree is probably due to the fact that it gives shade which is not obnoxious to the growth of grass.

All four species are subject to a great amount of variation, and in nurserymen's catalogues these forms have appropriate names, but they are not regarded as of sufficient permanence to merit scientific distinction. In point of age Elms are known to exceed five hundred years.

In October the leaves, which have for some time assumed a very dull dark-green tint, suddenly turn to orange, then fade to pale yellow, and fall in showers.

Among the insects that feed upon the Elm's foliage, the most noteworthy is the caterpillar of the Large Tortoiseshell Butterfly, and in our London parks and squares the Elms are much infested by the caterpillars of the Vapourer Moth, whose wingless females may be seen, like short-legged spiders, on the bark, whilst the male flutters in an apparently aimless way on wings of rich brown with central white spots.

The name Elm was derived from the Latin *Ulmus*, and appears to indicate an instrument of punishment—probably from its rods having been used to punish slaves.

THE LONDON PLANE

Family PLATANACEAE   *Platanus acerifolia*

In spite of the fact that the Plane is an exotic
of comparatively recent introduction, it seems
in a fair way of being associated in the future
with London. It has taken with great kind-
ness to London life, with all the drawbacks of
smoke, fog, flagstones, and asphalt. Its leaves

get thickly coated with grime, which also turns its light-grey bark to blackish ; but as the upper surface of the leaves is smooth and firm, a shower of rain washes them clean, and the rigid outer layer of bark is thrown off by the expansion of the softer bark beneath. This is not thrown off all at once, but in large and small flakes, which leave a smooth yellow patch behind, temporarily free from contamination. A large variety of trees has been tried for street- planting, but none has stood the trying conditions of

London so well as the London Plane (*P. acerifolia*), and therefore, before many years, the capital may well be the city of Planes.

The London Plane is believed to be of hybrid origin and to have first appeared about 1670 at Oxford. Some fine examples may be seen in

London parks and squares. It is not known anywhere in the wild state.

The London Plane normally rise to a height of something between seventy and ninety feet, and the trunk attains a circumference of from nine to twelve feet ; but there is a record of a Plane whose

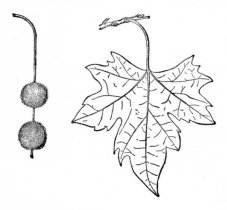

London Plane with fruits

waist measured twenty-five feet ! Many persons imagine because the leaves of the Plane resemble those of the Sycamore that the two are closely related; but a comparison of the flowers and fruit will show that this is not so. The catkins of the Plane take the form of balls, in which male *or* female flowers are pressed together; and the fruits, instead of being winged samaras, are the

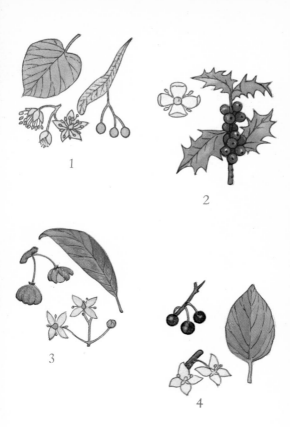

Pl. 1.   1. Lime.   2. Holly.   3. Spindle Tree.
4. Purging Buckthorn.

Pl. 2. 1. Horse Chestnut. 2. English Maple.
3. Sycamore. 4. Laburnum. 5. Locust.

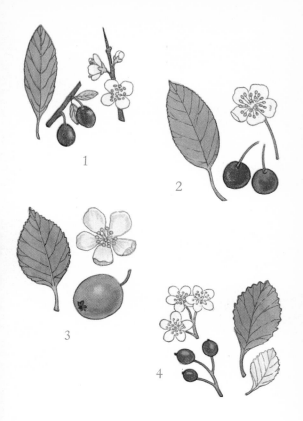

Pl. 3. 1. Sloe or Blackthorn. 2. Wild Cherry.
3. Wild Apple. 4. Whitebeam.

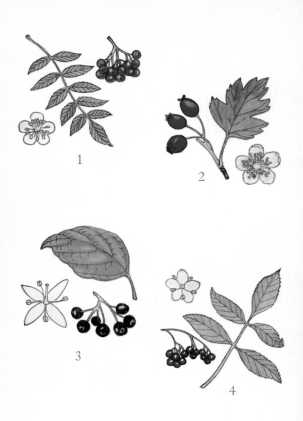

Pl. 4. 1. Mountain Ash. 2. Hawthorn.
3. Dogwood. 4. Elder.

Pl. 5.　1. Guelder Rose.　2. Wayfaring Tree.
3. Ash.　4. Bay Tree.

Pl. 6. 1. Box. 2. Wych Elm. 3. Elm.
4. Plane. 5. Walnut.

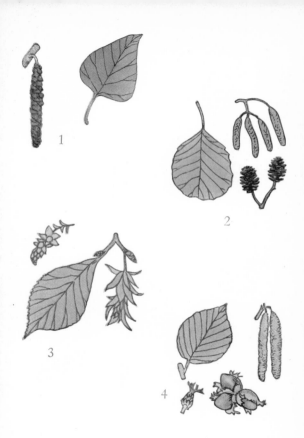

Pl. 7.   1. Birch.   2. Alder.   3. Hornbeam.
4. Hazel.

Pl. 8.   1. Oak.   2. Holm Oak.   3. Turkey Oak.
4. Sweet Chestnut.

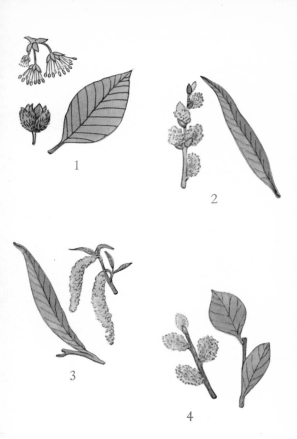

Pl. 9.   1. Beech.   2. Crack Willow.   3. White Willow
4. Sallow or Goat Willow.

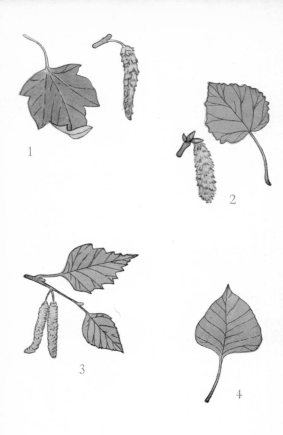

Pl. 10. 1. White Poplar. 2. Aspen Poplar.
3. Black Poplar. 4. Lombardy Poplar.

Pl. 11.   1. Yew.   2. Scots Pine.   3. Stone Pine.
4. Juniper.   5. Lawson's Cypress.

Pl. 12. 1. Larch. 2. Silver Fir. 3. Spruce.
4. Douglas Fir. 5. Cedar of Lebanon.

rough balls that so closely resemble an old-fashioned form of button, and the tree is known in some parts of the United States as the Button-wood.

The leaves are broad and five-lobed, and instead of being attached to the stem in pairs, as in the Sycamore, those of the Plane are alternate on opposite side of the shoot. In summer no buds can be seen because they are enclosed in the swollen bases of the leaf-stalks.

The outline of the tree is not so regular as in most others, the leaves being gathered in heavy masses, with broad spaces between, rather than equally distributed over the head. This is due to the freedom with which the crooked arms are flung about.

The pale-brown wood is fine-grained, tough, and hard, and is extensively used by coach-builders, cabinet-makers, etc., but is not highly esteemed for other purposes to which timber is put in this country.

THE WALNUT

Family J̃UGLANDACEAE   *J̃uglans regia*

The Walnut is a handsome tree, growing to a height of forty to a hundred feet, with a bole fifteen to eighteen feet in circumference, and a huge spreading head. The bark is of a cool-grey colour, smooth when young, but as the tree matures deep longitudinal furrows form, and it becomes very rugged. The twisted branches take a direction more upward than horizontal, but in early summer they are almost completely hidden by the masses of large and handsome leaves of warm-green colour and spicy aroma.

THE WALNUT

The large leaves are formed after the fashion of the Ash-leaf—broken up into a variable number of lance-shaped leaflets with entire or slightly wavy margins.

The flowering of the Walnut is much on the plan of the Oak and the Hazel, the sexes being in different flowers, but borne by one tree; the males forming a long drooping catkin, the females being solitary, or a few grouped at the end of a shoot. The males consist of a calyx of five greenish scales, enclosing a large number of stamens. The calyx of the female closely invests the ovary, which has two or three fleshy stigmas. Flowering takes place in early spring, before the leaf-buds have burst.

The fruit is a plum-like drupe, only the enveloping green flesh becomes brown, and splitting irregularly, discloses the " stone," which in this species takes the form of a hard but thin-shelled nut—the well-known Walnut, with its crinkled kernel of crisp, white flesh, from which a fine oil is obtained. The ripening of these nuts—which is accomplished by the beginning of October—can only be relied upon

A, female flowers ; B, male flowers.

in the southern half of Britain, and even there the crop is often spoiled by late frosts in spring.

Its chief value in Europe is as a fruit-tree, though the light but tough wood is much esteemed for the manufacture of furniture. Owing to its rapid growth, the grain is coarse, but the dark-brown colour is valued, especially as it is relieved by streaks and veins of lighter tints and black. It is easily worked, and bears a high polish.

THE WALNUT

The wood of young trees is white, gradually deepening to brown as maturity is approached. All the juices of the tree, whether from wood, bark, leaves, or green fruit, are rich in the brown pigment to which the colour of the timber is due. The combined lightness and toughness of the wood led to its adoption as the best material for making the stocks of guns and rifles. So great was the demand for this purpose, in the past, that large numbers of our finest Walnut trees were felled to provide the necessary timber. Some of these were doubtless the trees that were planted at Leatherhead in Surrey, also at Carshalton and Godstone in the same county, where the rambler may come across fine Walnut trees to this day, and occasionally find young ones growing wild in hedgerows and wastes.

The Walnut is a native of the Himalayas, Iran, Lebanon, and Asia Minor to Greece. The date of its introduction to Britain is usually set down as about the middle of the sixteenth century, but it was probably at least a century earlier, for it is recorded at the close of the sixteenth century, and described as a tree commonly to be seen in orchards, and in fields near the highways, where a very new importation was not likely to be found.

That the new importation was fully appreciated in Europe, in those early days, for its fruit, may be judged by the extent to which its cultivation was encouraged, and laws were enacted to preserve and increase the species, and those laws are inviolably observed to this day, for the extra-ordinary benefit the tree affords the inhabitants.

THE BIRCH

Family BETULACEAE   *Betula pendula*

    "The Lady of the Woods," as Coleridge christ-ened the Birch, is at once the most graceful, the hardiest, and the most ubiquitous of our forest trees. It grows throughout the length and breadth of our islands, and seems happy alike on a London common, in a suburban garden, or up

THE BIRCH

to an altitude of 2,500 feet in the Scottish highlands.

It penetrates farther north than any other tree, and its presence is a great boon to the natives of Lapland. It will grow where it is subjected to great heat, as well as where it must endure extreme cold, with its slender roots exploring the beds of peat, the rich humus of the old wood, or the raw soil of the mountainside, where it has to cling to rocks and a few mosses. Given plenty of light, it seems to care for little else.

Though a mere shrub in the far north, with us the Birch has a trunk sometimes as tall as eighty, but more frequently fifty feet, and a girth of from two to three feet. In its first decade it increases in height at the rate of a foot and a half to two feet a year ; but, of course, there is little breadth to be built up at the same time. It reaches maturity in half a century, and before the other half is reached the Birch will have passed away.

The bark of the Birch is more enduring than its timber, which may be partly due to its habit of casting off the outer layer in shreds, like fine tissue paper, from time to time. The greater

Birch leaves and ripening female catkins

part of the bark is silvery white, which adds to the apparent slenderness of the tree, and makes it conspicuous from a long distance; for the attenuated and drooping branches, dressed in small and loosely hung leaves, sway so constantly that the trunk is scarcely hidden.

The glossy, leathery leaves vary, from a triangular form to a pointed oval, their edges deeply toothed, and their foot-stalks long and slender.

About April the hanging catkins of the Birch, which were in evidence in the previous autumn, have matured and become dark crimson ; the scales separate and expose the two stamens of each flower, which has a single sepal. The female flowers are in a short, more erect spike, which consists of overlapping scales, each containing two or three flowers. These flowers have neither petals nor sepals, consisting merely of an ovary with two slender styles. After fertilization the female spike has developed into a little oblong cone. The minute nuts have a pair of delicate wings to each, and as they are set free from the cones they flutter on the breeze like a swarm of small flies. The moss that usually covers the ground beneath the Birch will be found, in October, to be thickly speckled with these fruits, which are something more than seeds ; they are really analogous to the acorn—a nut within a thin shell.

The tree sometimes begins to produce seed when only fifteen years old ; but as a rule, it is ten years older before it bears, and thereafter has a crop every year.

Birch-bark is used for tanning certain kinds of leather, and the peculiar odour of " Russian leather " is said to be due to the use of Birch in its preparation. The Birch agrees with the Beech in two respects—it is of little value for timber, but as a nurse to young timber-trees it is of considerable importance.

B. pendula is sometimes called the Warty Birch because of the little warts or swellings on its twigs, a feature which distinguishes it from the other common species of Birch found in Britain, the Hairy Birch, *B. pubescens*, in which the warts are absent and the twigs are downy; in old trees the bark of *B. pubescens* peels off in strips.

THE ALDER

Family BETULACEAE   *Alnus glutinosa*

Although the Alder is abundant by river-sides
and in all low-lying moist lands as far north as
Caithness, it is not so generally well known at
sight as the Oak, the Beech, and the Birch.

It is a small tree, ordinarily only thirty to forty
feet in height, with a girth from three to six feet,

though occasionally it reaches a hundred feet in height. This is when it is growing in moist loam, upon which rain or floods have washed down good layers of humus from woods at a higher elevation. If, with its roots thus cared for, its head is in a humid atmosphere, the Alder is in happy case. If it has had the misfortune to get into a porous soil, though this may be moist enough to please the Ash, the Alder becomes merely a big bush.

The bark of the Alder is rough and black, and the leaves, from two to four inches long, are roundish with a wedged-shaped base. They have a waved and toothed margin, and have short stalks. They remain green long after the leaves of other trees have fallen. In their young condition these leaves are covered with hairs, and are sticky to the touch, and when older they retain a distinct suggestion of greasiness. There are bacteria nodules on the roots.

The flowering of the Alder is similar to that of the Birch, but the male catkins have red scales, and each flower four stamens. These catkins are erect at first, afterwards becoming lax and drooping. The female spikes remain erect and have the fleshy scales covered by red-brown bracts.

Alder, with stalked bud, male catkins (above) and cones

Seed is not produced until the Alder is twenty years old, and the crop is repeated almost every year after. The cones are ripe about October and November, when they scatter their fruit, but the empty ones persist in hanging to the branches throughout the winter in numbers sufficient to give the leafless tree a brown appearance from a little distance. The immature male catkins are in evidence at the same time.

THE ALDER

The wood of the Alder is soft. Whilst the tree is alive its wood is white, but when cut and exposed to the air it becomes red; finally, on drying, it changes to a pinkish tint.

As timber it has no great reputation, except for piles or other submerged purposes, when it is said to be exceedingly durable. It has also enjoyed a great reputation for making the best charcoal for the gunpowder mills, and it is largely used by the wood-turner, the wood-carver, and the cabinet-maker.

There is a variety (*incisa*) of the Alder in which the leaves are so deeply toothed that they bear a close resemblance to those of the Hawthorn.

In some localities the tree is called the Howler and Aller; the latter word apparently is from the original Anglo-Saxon name.

THE HORNBEAM

Family BETULACEAE   *Carpinus betulus*

The Hornbeam appears to be a real native of
the south-east and midland counties of England,
and possibly of Wales. A line drawn from
Worcestershire to Norfolk roughly marks the
limit; north of that line the Hornbeam appears
to have been planted, as also in Ireland.

THE HORNBEAM

As an indigenous species it has had some doubts thrown upon it because there are some records of specimens having been introduced during the fifteenth century, but that is not sufficient ground upon which to deny nationality. Persons have been known to bring home from distant parts, as treasures, wild plants and ferns that were growing within a few miles of their own homes.

The Hornbeam is frequently passed by as a Beech, to which it has a very close superficial likeness, but a comparison of leaves, flowers, or bole would at once make the differences obvious. It is usually found in similar situations to the Beech, though it does not ascend so far up the hills as that species. On dry, poor soil it does not attain its full proportions and may only be classed as a small tree ; but when growing on low ground, in rich loam or good clay, it reaches a height of seventy feet, with a girth of ten feet. If two measurements of the bole's diameter be taken at right angles to each other, they will be found to differ greatly. A section of the trunk will not show a circular outline, but rather an ellipse, the bole appearing to have been flattened on two sides.

The bole is coated with a smooth grey bark, usually spotted with white.

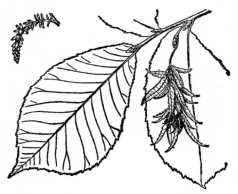

Male flowers above, fruits on right

The leaves are less symmetrical than those of Beech, and are of rougher texture, hairy on the underside, and their edges are doubly toothed. In autumn they turn yellow, then to ruddy gold, but a few days later they have settled into the rusty hue they retain throughout the winter, in those cases where they remain on the tree until spring.

THE HORNBEAM

The two kinds of catkins are similar and cylindrical, but whilst the male is pendulous from the beginning, the female is erect until after the formation of the fruit, when it gradually assumes the hanging position. The bracts of the male are oval, with sharp tips, each containing from three to twelve stamens. In the female the bracts fall early, but their place is taken by three-lobed bracteoles, which enlarge after flowering and become an inch or an inch and a half long. A single flower occupies each bracteole, consisting of a two-celled ovary and two styles. Only one cell develops, so that the hard green fruit contains but one seed.

The appearance of these fruits in autumn as they hang in a spray from the underside of the branches is quite distinct from those of any other of our native trees.

The wood is exceedingly tough, and not to be worked up with ease, but it is considered to make admirable fuel. It is said to burn like a candle. The carpenter is not pleased who has hornbeam to work up, for his tools lose their edge far too quickly for his labour to be profitable.

THE HAZEL

Family CORYLACEAE   *Corylus avellana*

It is rarely that the Hazel is allowed in this country to develop into a tree ; as a rule it is a shrub, forming undergrowth in wood or copse, or part of a hedge. As it is cut down with the copse or hedge, it cannot form a standard of any size. But that the Hazel left alone will develop into a small tree is shown by an example in East-well Park, Kent, whose height some years ago was thirty feet, with a circumference of three feet round the bole.

The large, roundish, heart-shaped leaves are arranged alternately in two rows along the straight downy shoots. Their margins are doubly toothed, and when in the bud they are

Upper, female flowers ; lower, male flowers.

plaited, the folds being parallel to the midrib. Soon after the buds open, many of the leaves assume a purplish tint for a while ; in autumn they turn brown, and finely pale or yellow.

Before the leaves appear the Hazel is rendered conspicuous by the male catkins, which are familiar to country children under the name of Lamb's-tails. These may be seen in an undeveloped condition in the autumn, when the nuts are being sought. A cluster of two or three hard, little grey-green cylinders is all that may then be seen of them ; but throughout the winter they lengthen, their scales loosen, and in February they are a couple of inches long, pliant, and yellow with the abundant pollen which blows out of them as they swing in the breeze.

The female flowers are by no means conspicuous, and have to be looked for. They will be found in the form of swollen buds on the upper part of the shoots and branches, from which issue some fine crimson threads. These are the styles and stigmas, and on dissection of the bud-like head, each pair of styles will be seen to spring from a two-celled ovary nestling between the bracts or scales of which the head is composed.

It is only rarely that the seed-egg in each cell develops ; as a rule one shrivels, and the other develops into the sweet " kernel" of the Hazel-nut. The shell is the ovary that has become woody and hard ; the ragged-edged leathery " shuck " is the enlarged bracts that surrounded the minute flower.

The Hazel likes a good soil, and will not really flourish without it, though it will *grow* almost anywhere, except where the moisture is stagnant.

Its wood is said to be best when grown on a chalky subsoil. As timber, the Hazel does not count, but its tough and pliant rods are valuable for many small uses, such as the making of hoops for casks, walking sticks, and—divining-rods ! The bark is smooth and brown.

The Barcelona nut, imported in winter, is only a variety of the Hazel ; as are also the Cob and Filbert, so largely cultivated in Kent.

THE OAKS

Family FAGACEAE *Quercus*

The Oak is the largest and longest-lived of our native trees and a very familiar object in the landscape in most parts of the British Isles. The sturdy, massive trunk, the broad, rounded outline of its head, its wide-spreading lower limbs, the wavy form of its leaves, and the egg-and-cup-shaped fruit, are characters that cannot be confused with any other tree.

The human centenarian is regarded with reverence, although he may have nothing beyond his great age to commend him ; but we think of the long period of history of which he has been a spectator, possibly an active maker of history. The huge Oak has probably lived through several such periods. Compared with the Oak, man is but of mushroom growth. Not till a century and a half have passed over its head is its timber fit for use, and as a rule it is not felled under the age of two hundred years. Many oaks are left to a much greater age, or we should not have still

with us so many venerable specimens, and where they have not been left until partially decayed, the timber is found to be still very valuable when finally cut down.

One of these patriarchs of the forest, known as the Gelenos Oak, standing about four miles from Newport, Monmouthshire, was cut down in 1810, and yielded 2,426 cubic feet of sound timber, and six tons of bark, which realized about £600. The timber and bark from this one tree were about equal to the average produce of three acres of oak coppice after fifteen years' growth.

THE OAKS

The Oak is most abundant on clay soils, but is at its best when growing in deep sandy loam, where there is also plenty of humus. Its roots, in such soil, strike down to a depth of about five feet.

Full - grown, it varies in height from sixty to one hundred and thirty feet, the difference depending upon situation; the tallest being those that have been drawn up in forests, at the expense of their branches. Trees growing freely in the open are of less height, and are made to appear comparative dwarfs by the huge  proportions of the bole. In the forest this may be up to ten feet in girth, but in isolated specimens, may be as much as thirty-six feet.

The thick, rough bark is deeply furrowed in a large network pattern, which affords temporary hiding-places for many kinds of insects. The

Oak is more persistently attacked by insects than any other tree, and one authority has tabulated about five hundred that get their living, mainly or entirely, from their attacks on the foliage, bark, or timber. With some species this warfare is waged so extensively that in some years, by early

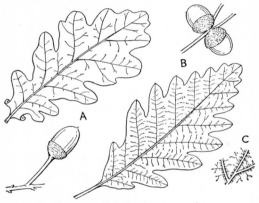

A. Common Oak (leaf and acorn)
B. Sessile Oak (leaf and acorn)
C. Sessile Oak (underside showing hairs)

summer, the trees are almost divested of their foliage, and a new crop of leaves becomes a necessity. But the reserve forces of the Oak are quite equal to this drain, and the tree does not appear to suffer.

The Oak flowers in April or May and the blossoms are of two distinct forms—male and female. The males are borne at intervals along a hanging stalk, two or three inches in length. They are green and inconspicuous. The female flowers are fewer, and will be found on short erect

Holm Oak.

stalks above the male catkins. Each female flower consists of a calyx, invested with a number of overlapping scales, and enclosing an ovary with three styles. The ovary is divided into three cells, each containing two seed-eggs. An acorn should therefore contain six kernels, but, as a rule, only one of the seed-eggs develops. The overlapping scales at the base of the female flower become the rough cup that holds the acorn.

Under the name " Common Oak " two distinct species, *Quercus robur*, Pedunculate Oak, and *Q. petraea*, Sessile or Durmast Oak, are included. The former is most abundant in the south of England, occurring as a native tree in the deeper, heavier soils. *Q. petraea* is common in the west and north on shallower and more sandy soils. *Q. robur* may easily be distinguished by the presence of two lobes at the base of each leaf. The leaves are almost stalkless and without hairs; the female flowers and acorns are borne on long stalks. In *Q. petraea*, the female flowers and acorns are stalkless and each leaf has a stalk; the leaves, moreover, have minute star-shaped hairs on their under surface. Hybrids between the two are of widespread occurrence.

Several Oaks of foreign origin are also grown in our parks and open spaces ; among them the Holm Oak (*Quercus ilex*) whose evergreen leaves have toothed or plain edges, and occasionally the lower ones develop holly-like marginal spines. It has a much thinner, more even bark than our native Oak, and of a black colour.

The Turkey Oak (*Quercus cerris*) is a much larger tree, attaining similar heights to our British species, but more pyramidal in form and with thick, greyish bark. The stalkless acorn-cups are covered with mossy scales, and the whole tree is of straighter growth, and the branches are not so gnarled and twisted as *Quercus robur*.

THE SWEET CHESTNUT

Family FAGACEAE   *Castanea sativa*

Until about the middle of the last century the Chestnut was generally regarded as a genuine native of the British Isles. It is now agreed that its real home is in Asia Minor and Greece, whence it was introduced to Italy in very remote times, and has since spread over most of temperate Europe.

In suitable situations the Chestnut is of larger

proportions and greater length of life than the Oak. In the South of England it will attain a height of from sixty to eighty feet in fifty or sixty years, and if g r o w i n g in d e e p, porous loam it builds up an erect massive column. Under l e s s suitable c o n ditions the undivided trunk is little more than ten feet long ; then it divides off into several h u g e limbs, and so the general character of the tree is altered. The branches have a horizontal and downward habit of growth, the extremities of the lower ones often being but little above the earth.

The fine elliptical leaves are nine or ten inches in length and of a rich green colour. Their edges

are cut into long pointed teeth. Towards the
autumn they pale to light yellow, and then deepen
into gold on their way to the final brown of the
fallen leaf, which, by the way, is a great enricher
of the soil.

The flowers, though individually small and

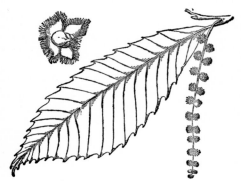

Sweet Chestnut in flower;
above fruit, showing nuts and husk

inconspicuous, are rather striking, from their
association in cylindrical yellow catkins, about
six inches long, which hang from the axils of the
leaves. The catkins arising from the axils of the
lower leaves of the twigs are composed entirely of
male flowers. Those arising from the upper
leaves consist of both sexes. The free end of this
type consists of male flowers, each with a number
of stamens enclosed in a calyx of five or six green
leaves.

THE SWEET CHESTNUT

The female flowers, nearer the base of the catkin, are two or three together in a prickly four-lobed involucre, and consist each of a calyx closely investing a tapering ovary, whose summit bears from five to eight radiating stigmas, the number corresponding with the cells into which the ovary is divided. Each cell contains two seed-eggs, but as a rule only one in each flower develops, and ultimately the involucre entirely surrounds the seed cluster with the hedgehog-like coat in which the nuts are contained when ripe. Then it splits open and discloses the two or three glossy brown nuts. The Chestnut is in flower from May to July, and the nuts drop in October. They form an important article of food in Southern Europe, where they are produced in abundance.

The trees begin to bear when about twenty-five years old, and from thence on to the fiftieth or sixtieth year the timber is at its best. The young wood is covered with smooth brown bark, becoming grey later, and its surface splits into longitudinal fissures. In older trees the fissures have a distinct spiral twist, which gives the tree the appearance of having been wrenched round by some mighty force. The average age of the Chestnut is about five hundred years, but there have been in this country many trees that were much older.

THE BEECH

Family FAGACEAE *Fagus sylvatica*

To the Beech the title of " Mother of Forests " has been given, and the grower of timber freely acknowledges his heavy indebtedness to this nursing mother, for, in the words of Professor Gayer, the Bavarian forestry expert, " without Beech there can no more be properly tended forests of broad-leaved genera, as along with it would have to be given up many other valuable timber-trees, whose production is only possible with the aid of Beech."

Quite apart from utilitarian considerations, it would be very sad to lose the Beech, with its towering, massive shaft clad in smooth grey bark, its spreading roots above the soil, and the dense shade of its fine foliage. Fortunately for the lover of natural beauty, it is this luxuriant growth of leaves and the shade it gives that are the redeeming virtues of the Beech in the eye of the forester.

Its drip destroys most of the soil-exhausting weeds, its shade protects the soil from over-evaporation, and the heavy crop of leaves enriches it by their decomposition.

The well-grown Beech attains a height of about one hundred feet, with a girth of twenty feet. It will grow in most upland places, where the Oak thrives, though it does not need so deep a soil, and has a preference for land containing lime. Fresh mineral soils, rich in humus, are the best for it. In poor soils its growth is slow and its life is longer. It begins to bear mostly at about eighteen years of age, and thereafter gives good crops at intervals of three or five years.

In spring, just before the buds expand, the twigs of the Beech have a very distinct appearance. The buds are long and slender, placed alternately along the twig, and the brown scales retain their shape long after they have been cast off. In the bud the leaf is folded fanwise, and the folds run parallel with the nerves. They expand into an oval, smooth-faced leaf, with slightly scooped edges, and a most delicate fringe of short gossamer, which falls off later. These leaves are rich in potash, and as they readily decay, they produce an admirable humus. In sheltered places the leaves, turned to a light ruddy-brown colour, are retained on the lower branches until cast off by the expansion of the new buds.

In early summer, whilst the leaves are still pellucid, the shade of a big Beech is particularly inviting. Later the leaves become opaque, and their glossy surfaces throw back the heat rays. Then the play of light upon the great mass of foliage is very fine; but when autumn has turned their deep green to orange and warm ruddy-brown, and they catch the red rays of the westering sun, the tree appears to be turned into a blazing fire.

The Beech flowers in April or May. The blossoms of the male flowers are gathered together in a hanging purplish-brown rounded tassel with yellow anthers. The female flowers, to the number of two, three, or four, are clustered in a "cupule" of overlapping scales, like those of the Oak. But in the Beech the "cupule"

becomes a bristly closed box, which afterwards opens by one end splitting into four triangular silk-hair-lined valves, which turn back and reveal the three-sided, sharp-edged " mast." This " mast " was formerly a very valuable product of the Beech-woods, when herds of swine

A, female ; B, male flowers.

were turned in to feed upon the fallen Beech-nuts. Beech-mast is still a good food eagerly taken by such woodland creatures as deer, badgers, squirrels, and dormice.

The vitality of the Beech is so high that frequently the bole divides at its upper part into several trunks, which rise straight up, and each attains the dimensions of a complete tree. Often such a tree stands on a sandy bank, and seems in imminent danger of toppling over, but its up-rightness secures it against strain, and the roots that it sent down the steep sides of the bank have thickened into strong props.

As the value of the Beech as a nurse for other trees, and its frequent use for that purpose, have been mentioned, it should also be stated that it is a powerful competitor with other trees, and if these are left to fight their own battles unaided, the Beech will be the conqueror. John Evelyn pointed out, over two centuries ago, that where mixed woods of Oak and Beech were left to them-selves, they ultimately became pure Beech woods. The Beech appears to gain this advantage through rooting in the surface soil, and, exhausting it of food elements, suffers none to penetrate to the lower strata, where the Oak has its roots.

The Copper Beech which is so effectively used for ornament in parks and gardens, is merely a variety of the Common Beech, and all the examples in cultivation are believed to be " sports " from the purple variety, which itself was a natural sport discovered in a German wood more than a hun-dred years ago.

THE WILLOWS

Family SALICACEAE   *Salix*

In their natural condition Willows are graceful and picturesque, but a large number of the examples met with have been so altered for commercial reasons as to be more grotesque than beautiful. The pollard Willow, though it produces a shock-head of long, slender shoots, lets in moisture at the top of the bole, and the wood is more or less decayed and worthless.

Only four of our native Willows can be regarded as timber-trees. These are the White Willow, the Crack Willow, the Bedford Willow, and the Sallow. Like the Poplars, their growth is very rapid, and their wood is consequently light. In the present day the growers of straight-boled Willows find their best market among the makers of cricket-bats. A good deal of it is also cut into thin strips for plaiting into hand-baskets. The Osier is grown in extensive riverside beds for the production of long, pliant shoots for the basket-weavers ; though many of the so-called Osier rods are really stool-shoots from Willows that have been pollarded, or whose leading shoot has never been allowed to grow. On those parts of our coast where the crab and lobster fishery is pursued, a regular supply of such shoots for weaving into " pots " is a necessity.

The bark of the tree Willows has long been known to be rich in an alkaloid called *salicine*, which has tonic and astringent properties. It is also used in tanning.

Almond-leaved Willow.

The Almond-leaved or French Willow (*Salix triandra*) is a small tree about twenty feet high, distinguished by its bark being thrown off in flakes. Its slender, lance-shaped leaves are smooth, green above and glaucous beneath, two to four inches long, and with heart-shaped stipules. The male flowers are distinguished by their stamens being three in number. Its habitats are the banks of rivers and streams, and in Osier-beds. It is extensively grown on account of the long, straight shoots produced from the stump when the tree is cut down, which are of great use in wicker-work.

The Bay-leaved Willow (*Salix pentandra*) is met with either as a small upright tree about twenty feet high, or as a shrub eight feet high. Its oval

Bay-leaved Willow.

or elliptical leaves are rich green, smooth and sticky on the upper surface, and give out a pleasant fragrance like those of the Bay-tree; they vary from an inch to four inches long, and they may or may not bear stipules, but if these are present they will be egg-shaped or oblong.

The stamens are normally five in each flower, but they vary up to twelve. This species is reputed to be, of all our Willows, the latest to flower.

A line drawn through York, Worcester, and North Wales will give roughly its southward range as a native species. South of that line it has been planted ; north of it to the Scottish border it is a native. It has been found growing in North-umberland at a height of thir-teen hundred feet.

Bole of Bay-leaved Willow.

The Crack Willow or Withy (*Salix fragilis*) is one of the two most considerable of our tree Willows. In good soil it will in twenty years attain nearly its full height, which is about seventy feet. Its bole sometimes has a girth of twenty feet. Its smooth, polished shoots afford the best

Crack Willow.

ready means of distinguishing it, for instead of
their base pointing to the centre of the trunk,
as in other trees, they grow obliquely, so that
the shoots frequently cross each other. They are
both tough and pliant, but if struck at the base,

they readily break off. This character explains the names Crack Willow and *fragilis*.

The leaves are lance-shaped, three to six inches long, smooth, with glandular teeth, pale or glaucous on the underside, and with half - heart - shaped stipules, w h i c h, however, are soon cast off.

The male and female catkins of the Willows are borne by different trees. In the case of the Crack Willow, the male catkins are about two inches long, proportionately stout, each flower bearing two stamens (occasionally three, four, or five). The female catkin is more slender, the flowers each containing a smooth ovary, ending in a short style that divides into two

Bole of Crack Willow.

curved bilobed stigmas. The catkins appear in April or May.

Like most of the Willows, this species is fond of cold, wet soil in low situations, but it is not restricted to the plains. In Northumberland it is found at 1,300 feet above sea-level. Its north-ward range extends as far as Ross-shire, but it is a doubtful native in both Scotland and Ireland.

White Willow.

The White Willow (*Salix alba*) is so called from the appearance of the leaves as the light is reflected from their silky surfaces. It is a tree from sixty to eighty feet high, with a girth of about twenty feet, covered with thick and deeply fissured bark.

THE WILLOWS

The leaves are from two to four inches long, of a narrow, elliptical shape. In the typical form the twigs are olive-coloured, but in the variety *vitellina* (known as the Golden Willow) these are yellow or reddish. The Golden Willow has less hairy and narrower leaves than the White Willow. The White Willow is found as far north as Sutherlandshire, but although it is believed to be an indigenous species, most of the modern specimens appear to have been planted. It affords good timber, and the bark is almost equal to that of Oak for tanning.

A great number of the old Willows met with are partially decayed, a condition frequently the result of lopping large branches, for the wound never heals and decay sets in.

Bole of White Willow.

The Bedford Willow (*Salix viridis*) is believed

to be a hybrid between the Crack Willow and the White Willow. It grows to a height of fifty feet with a girth of twelve feet. The leaves are more slender than those of the Crack Willow, taper to a point at each end, and are very smooth on both sides. It occurs in swampy woods.

The Cricket-bat Willow (*Salix alba* var. *coerulea*) is a variety of the White Willow. It differs in its pyramidal habit and its less hairy and thinner leaves. It is quick growing and reaches a height of a hundred feet. The wood is elastic and tough and is the most suitable for making cricket-bats.

The Sallow or Goat Willow (*Salix caprea*) is the only other species that can properly be considered as a tree, as it attains to a height of forty feet, though fifteen to twenty feet is more common.

Its usually egg-shaped leaves vary from almost round to elliptical or lance-shaped, and from two to four inches in length. In the typical form, which occurs chiefly in woods, dry pastures, and hedgerows, they are broad, smooth, and light-green above, covered with soft white down beneath ; the stipules are half-kidney-shaped.

This is the earliest of all our Willows to flower, and the gold (male) and silver (female) catkins are put out before the leaves.

Those who imagine that insect life is suspended until spring is on the verge of summer should visit the woods when the Sallow is in bloom ; they will be astonished at the swarms of bees and moths that are collecting the abundant pollen or sipping the nectar provided for them.

THE WILLOWS

The all but invariable rule among the Poplars —as among Oak, Beech, Birch, Hazel, and Pine— is to depend upon the wind for the transfer of pollen from one tree to the stigmas of another of the same species, but in the Willows we find a

Almond-leaved Willow ; Bay-leaved Willow ; Sallow ; Crack Willow ; White Willow.

breaking away from what was doubtless the primitive arrangement in all flowering plants, by the bribing with nectar of more reliable and less wasteful winged carriers.

The Grey Sallow (*Salix cinerea*) is a close relative of *S. caprea* but it has hairy and rather blackish twigs and buds. The leaves are smaller and narrower and the margins are often slightly inrolled. It is the commonest and most widely spread species of Willow in the British Isles.

The Eared Sallow (*Salix aurita*) is distinguished by its small, bush-like proportions (two to four feet high), long branches, and red twigs; its small wrinkled leaves, which are usually less than two inches long, are of almost oblong shape, downy beneath, and with large ear-shaped stipules. It is fond of the acid soil of damp copses and moist places on heaths, where it may be found at considerable elevations.

There are Willows of dwarf habit, some with long straggling branches and more or less prosstrate stems, that grow upon heaths.

The Creeping Willow (*Salix repens*). One form or another of this species will be found in all parts of the British Islands where there are heaths and commons; in the Highlands it occurs as high as 2,500 feet.

It is a low bush from six to twelve inches high, the stem lying along the ground. Some of the branches straggle in the same fashion, but those which bear the flowers are more or less erect. The leaf-buds and the young leaves are silky. They are broadly or narrowly lance-shaped; in size from a half to one and a half inches in length, and may have lance-shaped stipules, or none at all. The scales of the catkins are yellowish-green or purple, with dark tips. After they have shed their pollen the anthers turn black.

Another group of small Willows that form bushes have been united under two species—the Dark-leaved Willow (*Salix nigricans*) and the Tea-leaved Willow (*Salix phylicifolia*). None of them occur south of Yorkshire, and the chief

distinction between them consists in the leaves of
S. nigricans turning black when dried, whilst
those of *S. phylicifolia* do not.

The Osier (*Salix viminalis*).   Many of the fore-
going Willows, when cut down low and induced

Osier: male catkins on left

to send out long, slender shoots, are known as
Osiers, but only two species are botanically
regarded as Osiers—this and the Purple Osier
(*Salix purpurea*).

The present species may remain as a shrub or
grow into a small tree, thirty feet high, with long,
straight branches, which are silky when young,
but afterwards become polished.   The leaves
vary in length from four to ten inches, and are
lance-shaped, tapering to a point at the top and

Purple Osier.

narrowing into the foot-stalk at the base. They have waved margins without teeth, and the upper surface netted with veins, the under surface silvery and silky; stipules lance-shaped.

The Osier may be seen in Osier-beds and wet

places generally throughout the country as far north as Elgin and Argyll.

The Purple Osier (*Salix purpurea*) gets its name from the red or purple bark which clothes the thin but tough twigs. It is a shrub, growing from five to ten feet high. The leaves, which are rather thin in texture, are from three to six inches long, of slender lance-shape, with toothed edges, smooth and glaucous on both sides. They are almost opposite on the twigs. There are several varieties of this shrub.

There remains a group of several small species of very local occurrence.

The Whortle-leaved Willow (*Salix myrsinites*) is a small, wiry, creeping, or half-erect shrub, six inches to a foot high, with toothed, dark glossy leaves, an inch or less in length, whose net-veining shows on both sides. It is restricted to the Alpine parts of mid-Scotland, from 1,000 to 2,700 feet.

The Small Tree-Willow (*Salix arbuscula*) is a small shrub, whose stem creeps along the ground and roots as it goes, sending up more or less erect branches a foot or two high. The downy twigs are yellow at first, then reddish-brown. The small toothed leaves are shining above and glaucous beneath. It grows in the highlands of Aberdeen, Argyll, Dumfries, Forfar, and Perth on ground between 1,000 and 2,400 feet.

The Weeping Willow (*Salix babylonica*), so popular an ornament of riverside lawns, is not a

Weeping Willow.

native tree. Its slender hanging branches make it a conspicuous feature of the banks of the upper Thames. It grows to a height of thirty to fifty feet and has large, lance-shaped leaves, dark green above and glaucous beneath. The female tree, which is much more common than the male, has two-inch long catkins appearing in April with the leaves.

THE WILLOWS

The Weeping Willow was given the name of *babylonica* because it was thought to be a native of the region of the Euphrates and to be the Willow referred to in the Psalms. It is really a native of China, but it has long been cultivated in Eastern Europe, North Africa, and Western Asia, and was probably introduced into England during the eighteenth century. Napoleon was very fond of this tree and its greatly increased popularity shortly after his death was said to be due to the introduction of young Weeping Willows raised from the tree under which he was buried at St. Helena.

The Dwarf Willow (*Salix herbacea*) is not restricted in its range, for it is found in all parts of the United Kingdom, where there are heights sufficiently Alpine (2,000 to 4,300 feet) for its tastes. It is only an inch or two high, and has consequently the distinction of being *the smallest British willow*. Its shrubby stem and branches creep along underground, sending up only short, scantily leaved twigs. The curled, roundish leaves do not exceed half an inch in length ; they are net-veined, toothed, and shining. The catkins appear after the leaves.

The Net-leaved Willow (*Salix reticulata*) is another of the Scotch Alpines. It is similar in habit to *S. herbacea*, but larger, its buried branches sending up twigs a foot long. The roundish, oblong, leathery leaves are not toothed ; they are smooth above and glaucous beneath, strongly net-veined on either side. The purplish or yellow catkins do not develop till after the leaves. It is restricted to the mountains of Merionethshire, Aberdeen, Forfar, Inverness, Perth and Sutherland.

The Woolly Willow (*Salix lanata*) is a small shrub, two or three feet high, with twisted branches, woolly twigs, and hairy black buds. The leaves are broad, egg-shaped and leathery, two or three inches long. There are half-heart-shaped stipules at the base of the very short leaf-stalk.

It is an Alpine plant, and is found about the mountain rills of Perth, Forfar, Inverness, and Sutherland at elevations between 2,000 and 2,500 feet. It is conspicuous in spring for its rich golden catkins.

Sadler's Willow (*Salix sadleri*), of which only two or three specimens have been found, is probably a form of *S. lanata*.

The Lapland Willow (*Salix lapponum*) is of similar proportions to *S. lanata*, sometimes erect, sometimes trailing. Its leaves are more elliptic in shape. In *S. lanata* the raised veins form a network pattern ; in *S. lapponum* they are straight. The stipules are small or altogether wanting. It is restricted to Scotch Alpine rocks, at elevations between 2,000 and 2,700 feet.

THE POPLARS

Family SALICACEAE   *Populus*

Six kinds of Poplar are commonly grown in this country, of which three are regarded as indigenous species. These are the Aspen, the Grey Poplar, and the Black Poplar. Then, of common introduced species, we have the White Poplar, the Lombardy Poplar and the hybrid Black Italian Poplar.

The Poplars share the love of the Willows for moist places. Their growth is rapid, and their timber, consequently, is of little value, though its softness and lightness render it suitable for many uses, such as box-making and flooring. An additional point in favour of White Poplar for the latter purpose is its unreadiness to burn.

The Poplars and the Willows agree broadly in the construction of their flowers in catkins, but whereas the Poplars have broad leaves and drooping catkins, the Willows, with few exceptions, have long, slender leaves and erect catkins. The sexes are not only in distinct flowers, but on separate trees, and the males appear to be far more numerous than the females. In the popular sense there are no flowers, for there are neither sepals nor petals, each set of sexual organs being protected merely by a scale. The catkins usually appear before the leaves. As there is nothing to attract insects to the work, the Poplars have to rely upon the wind for conveying the pollen to the female trees.

White Poplar.

The White Poplar, or Abele (*Populus alba*), is not so tall a tree as the Grey Poplar, generally not exceeding fifty feet in this country. Covered with smooth grey bark, its branches spread horizontally, and its lobed, maple-like leaves are hung on long, slender foot-stalks, which are flattened at the sides, so that when moved by the wind they flutter laterally. The leaves vary in shape. Those on long vigorous shoots and suckers are large, triangular in shape and deeply lobed. They are slightly hairy on the upper surface and covered with a dense snow-white felt on the under side. The leaf buds and young twigs are similarly covered. The leaves on the short shoots are oval, less deeply lobed and often not so densely hairy on the under surface.

The catkins, which appear in March and April, are cylindrical ; those of the male trees are rarely, if ever, seen in Britain. The female catkins are about an inch long, the two yellow stigmas are slender, with slit tips, and the ovaries develop into slender egg-shaped capsules, each with its fringed scale.

Bole of White Poplar.

In July when the seed capsules open, the surrounding vegetation and ground are thickly strewn with the long, white cotton filaments attached to the seeds.

The wood of this tree is softer and more spongy

than that of other Poplars. This species is said not to produce flowers in Scotland.

White Poplar.

The Grey Poplar (*Populus canescens*), which is thought to be indigenous only in central and southern England, attains to eighty or ninety feet, with a girth of ten to twenty-four feet. Its life extends to about a century, but its wood is considered best between fifty and sixty years of age.

The leaves on the short shoots are shaped like those of the White Poplar, but their undersides are either coated with grey down or are quite smooth ; those of the long shoots have their margins cut into angles and teeth. The female flowers mostly have four wedge-shaped purple stigmas, cleft into four at their extremities.

THE POPLARS

The Aspen (*Populus tremula*) does not attain either to so large a size or so moderate an age as

Aspen with male catkin

the Grey Poplar. Its height, when full-grown, is from forty to eighty feet ; but after fifty or sixty years its heart-wood begins to decay, and its destruction is then hastened even more by the attacks of such internal-feeding insects as the caterpillars of the Goat-moth and the Wood Leopard-moth.

The leaves on the branches are broadly egg-shaped, the waved margin cut into teeth with turned-in points. In one form (var. *villosa*) the leaves are covered beneath with silky or cottony hairs ; in the other form (var. *glabra*) they are almost smooth. The leaves on the suckers are heart-shaped, with glandular teeth. The leaf-stalks are longer than those of its congeners, so that they are constantly on the flutter.

The catkins, which are two or three inches long, are similar to those of the White and Grey Poplars, but the scales have jagged edges.

It is indigenous in all the British Islands as far north as Orkney, but, though commonly found in copses on a moist, light soil, is more frequent as a planted tree in gardens and pleasure grounds. It is a characteristic tree of the plains throughout the Continent, but ascends to 1,600 feet in Yorkshire, and in the Bavarian Alps is found as high as 4,400 feet. It is not deep-rooted, and the root-branches run almost horizontal. Where accessible to cattle and deer, the foliage of the suckers is eagerly browsed by them.

The Black Poplar (*Populus nigra*) appears to be so called, not by reason of any blackness of leaf or bark, but because of the absence of any white or grey down on the underside of its leaves. Its bark is grey, and readily distinguished by the great swellings and nodosities that mar the symmetry of its trunk.

It is a tree of erect growth, fifty or sixty feet in height, with horizontal branches, and leaves that vary in shape from triangular to almost circular, and in width from an inch to four inches. They have rounded teeth on the margins, and in their young state the underside is silky.

The flowers in the catkins are not densely packed. Those of the male are two or three inches in length, and dark red in colour; their

Black Poplar.

abundance before the tree has put out its leaves makes the male tree a conspicuous object. The female catkins are shorter and do not droop. When the roundish capsules burst in May or June to distribute their seeds, the white cotton with which the latter are invested gives prominence to the female tree.

The wood is chiefly used by the wood-turner; in Holland, where it is extensively cultivated, it provides the material for sabots.

The Black Poplar is indigenous in the eastern counties and in Wales. Some botanists regard the Lombardy Poplar as a variety of the Black Poplar, as apart from the very different habit of the tree—not by itself sufficient grounds for separation—there is little else to distinguish it.

Bole of Black Poplar.

The Lombardy Poplar (*Populus italica*) was for many years a tree of mysterious origin. It appeared in Italy about the middle of the eighteenth century, and was called Lombardy Poplar in consequence of its introduction thence by Lord Rochford in 1758. The original was a male tree, and as practically all of the vast number of Lombardy Poplars now existing have descended

Black Poplar.

from cuttings or suckers of that tree, they also are males. The general supposition is that the original tree arose as a sport from the Black Poplar. A few females are known to exist, and these are probably the offspring of a later crossing.

Its glossy leaves are shaped like those of the Black Poplar, but its branches, instead of spreading, all grow straight upwards, so that the spire-shape of the tree is produced—a shape only found otherwise among coniferous trees, particularly in the Cypress, the Juniper, and the Irish Yew.

It is its form, great height (80 to 100 feet), and

Lombardy Poplar.

rapidity of growth that have led to its wide use here as an ornamental tree. Its growth is extremely rapid, especially during its first twenty years, when it will attain a height of sixty feet or more, provided it be grown in good, moist (but not marshy) soil.

Its wood is, of course, of little value, and is chiefly used for making boxes and packing-cases.

The bark is rough and deeply furrowed; the furrows are spiral. Like the Black Poplar, it has smooth shoots, and the unopened buds are sticky.

The Black Italian Poplar (*Populus serotina*), appeared in the 18th century apparently as a result of the crossing of the Black Poplar with an American species (*P. deltoidea*).

The stem is free from the swellings and burrs of the Black Poplar and the ascending branches form a fan-like crown. The leaves are oval, about three inches broad, toothed and fringed, and appear later than any other Poplar.

Bole of Lombardy Poplar.

The Ontario or Balsam Poplar (*Populus candicans*) has broadly ovate leaves which are

Black Italian Poplar.

dark-green with few hairs on the upper surface and whitish on the lower surface. It produces many suckers.

The distinctive character of the tree is the fragrance of its young foliage, which scents the air on moist evenings, and makes it a desirable tree to plant near water.

THE CONIFERS

The British flora is singularly poor in coniferous plants, the Scots Pine, the Juniper, and the Yew being our only native species.

The principal feature distinguishing all Conifers and their allies (*Gymnosperms*) from other flowering plants (*Angiosperms*) is briefly this : Angiosperms have their incipient seeds (*ovules*) enclosed in a carpel, through which a shoot from the pollen grain has to penetrate in order to reach and fertilize the ovule. In Gymnosperms the carpel takes the form of a leaf or bract, upon which the naked ovule lies open to actual contact with the pollen grain. After fertilization the carpel enlarges to protect the seed, and becomes fleshy or woody, in the latter case a group of carpels forming the well-known cones of Pine or Fir.

In some of the groups the male or pollen-producing flowers are borne by a separate tree from that which bears the female or cone-producing flowers. In the Pines both sexes are found on the same tree ; and in all Conifers the pollen is carried by the wind. They are among the most valuable of timber trees, and, in addition, yield a number of useful substances, such as pitch, tar, turpentine, etc.

The linear leaves are always rigid, extremely narrow, and long in proportion, with the two sides parallel. In the Pines they are in clusters of two, three, or five, seeming to be bound together at the base by a wisp of thin skin. The number of leaves in each bundle is often a help in distinguishing species.

THE YEW

Family TAXACEAE   *Taxus baccata*

The Yew lacks the graceful proportions of most of our trees, but it has for compensation a most obvious air of strength and endurance.

Many people see in cathedral aisles the reproduction in stone of the pine-forest or the beech-wood. Standing before an ancient Yew they may see whence came the idea for those *clustered* columns. They actually exist in the bole of the Yew, which presents the appearance not of a single trunk, but of several trunks that have coalesced. This condition is due to the Yew continually pushing out new shoots from the lower part of its bole, which take an upright direction, and coalesce with the old wood.

Although the Yew is a large tree, it is by no means a tall tree ; the height of full-grown Yews in this country ranging between fifteen and fifty feet, though they are said to attain a greater length in India.

The bole of the Yew is short but massive, covered with thin red bark, that flakes off in patches much after the manner of Plane-bark. Large specimens have a girth of from twenty-five to fifty feet — or even more. Such a circumference represents the growth of many centuries, for the annual growth rings are very thin. It is this very slow growth that produces the hard, compact, and elastic wood that was

so highly esteemed in the past. Not only is the timber elastic, but it is exceedingly durable, so that it is said, " A post of Yew will outlast a post of iron." Its branches start from the trunk at only a few feet from the ground, and taking an almost horizontal direction, throw out a great number of leafy twigs, which provide a dense and extensive shade. The leaves are leathery in texture, curved somewhat after the manner of a reaping-hook, shiny and dark above, pale and unpolished below.

The Yew is a diœcious tree—that is, one whose

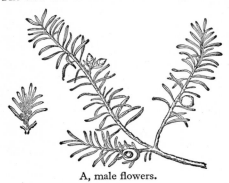

A, male flowers.

male and female blossoms are borne on separate trees—but the statement requires qualification to this extent, that occasionally a tree will be found bearing a branch or branches whose flowers are of the sex opposite to those covering the greater part of the tree.

The male flower is almost round, a quarter of an inch across, and contains about half a dozen yellow anthers, the base surrounded by dry overlapping scales. They may be found during February and March, in profusion on the underside of the boughs. The female flower is much smaller, and consists of a fleshy disk with a few scales at its base, and on this stands a single seed-egg. After fertilization of the seed-egg, the disk develops into a red wax-like cup around the enlarging seed with its olive-green coat. The flesh of the cup is full of sweet mucilage, which makes the fruit acceptable to children, but the flavour is rather too mawkish to suit older tastes. Yew-berries are not poisonous, as sometimes supposed, but the hard seed has undoubtedly poisonous properties.

Much has been said and written as to the toxic properties of Yew-leaves, and it appears that if eaten in large quantities they will prove fatal to man, cattle, horses, sheep, pigs, and possibly other animals, but small quantities of the leaves are usually harmless.

Along the chalk range of which the celebrated Box Hill forms part will be found many fine examples of the Yew, as at Cherkley Court, near Leatherhead, where there is an actual Yew forest.

It is reputed to be the longest-lived of all trees. It is naturally a tree of the uplands and lower hills, and shows a distinct preference for soils that contain plenty of lime.

The Irish Yew (var. *fastigiata*) differs from the type in having all its branches growing erectly, after the manner of a Lombardy Poplar, and in the leaves being scattered promiscuously over the branchlets instead of being in two regular rows. It attains a height of twenty to thirty-five feet.

THE SCOTS PINE

Family PINACEAE   *Pinus sylvestris*

The Scots Pine, commonly but incorrectly styled Scotch Fir, is the typical Pine-tree of Northern Europe, where it constitutes huge forests. Although in ancient days it was pretty widely distributed over Britain, to-day all those Pine-woods in Southern England are the result of planting, and it is only in the Highlands of Scotland that it can be regarded as truly wild and indigenous.

In favourable situations, the Scots Pine is a fine tree a hundred feet high, with a rough - barked trunk, whose girth is sometimes twelve feet. It develops a strong taproot, which goes deep ; but where the soil is shallow the taproot is not developed. At great elevations the upward growth is checked early. The branches are short and spreading, those on the lower portions of the trunk dying early, so that the tree soon gets that gaunt, weather-beaten look that is so characteristic of it. Its growth is rapid, and in twenty years it will attain a height of forty or fifty feet.

The leaves which are in bundles of two, are from two to four inches long, very slender, grooved above and convex beneath. They remain on the tree for over two years, and in their first season are of a glaucous hue, but in the second year this changes to dark deep-green.

Both male and female flowers are borne by the same tree. The male flowers are individually small (quarter of an inch), but are combined in

spikes; this and the abundant pale yellow pollen makes them conspicuous. The female cones are somewhat egg-shaped, tapering to a point, which is often curved. They are usually in clusters of three, and grow to a length of two or three inches. The scales are comparatively few, and their ends are thickened into a four-sided boss. The seeds are winged, and contained beneath the scales.

They take about eighteen months to ripen, when the scales separate in dry, windy weather, and allow the breeze to pick out the seeds and send them flying through the air to a great distance. The pollen, too, is of a form specially fitted for aerial transport, each particle of pollen forming two connected spheres. It is quite a common experience in May to find little heaps of this pale yellow pollen collected in hollows and at the margins of ponds in the neighbourhood of pine-woods.

Although the wood produced by the Scots Pine in this country is not considered of the highest quality, the species is certainly of equal value as a timber-producer with any other tree. Owing to our mild winters and long periods of seasonal growth, the Pine wood produced in Britain is coarse-grained and not very durable. In the colder parts of Northern Europe, where summers are short, and the long winters are severe, the texture of the timber is more solid and the grain closer.

In addition to the timber, other valuable substances, such as pitch and tar, resin, and turpentine, for example, are products of the Scots Pine.

Though it likes a deep soil in which to strike its tap-root, it will grow upon rocky ground, or it will form forests on poor sandy soils, even on the loose hot sands near the seashore. This is a very valuable power, because the fall of its needles gradually forms a humus, and so provides food for other plants which could not exist on raw sand.

THE AUSTRIAN PINE

Family PINACEAE   *Pinus nigra*

The range of the Austrian Pine and its varieties together includes Central and Southern Europe, and part of Western Asia. There is a variety known as the Corsican Pine, and its botanical name correctly set out is *Pinus nigra* var. *maritima.*

THE AUSTRIAN PINE

It is a comparatively recent addition to our sylva in both forms, for the Corsican Pine was introduced in 1759, in the belief that it was a maritime form of the Scots Pine, but the type was first sent out by Messrs. Lawson & Son, the Edinburgh nurserymen, in 1835.

The Corsican Pine is a slender tree of somewhat pyramidal form, growing to a height of eighty to one hundred and twenty feet. The Austrian Pine, though a large tree, is of smaller proportions — from sixty to eighty feet high — but with stouter and longer branches, and denser foliage.

The leaves, which vary from three to five inches in length, are sheathed in pairs, convex on the outer side, rigid, glossy, dark green, and with toothed margins. The cones are solitary or in clusters, ovoid-conic in shape, shining brown, two to three inches long, by an inch in diameter, straight or curved. They ripen in the spring or summer of the third year and fall off soon after the escape of the seeds.

Pinus nigra is a very variable species, including several geographical forms which differ in habit and density of foliage. The species may generally be distinguished amongst two-leaved pines by its yellowish-brown shoots, stout leaves, ovoid, abruptly pointed buds, and tawny-yellow cones.

Pinus nigra and its varieties will thrive in pure sand and on that account make excellent seaside trees. The Austrian Pine when exposed to strong sea winds develops a dense branch system, which affords a good wind break, and it is therefore useful as a shelter belt. It also grows vigorously in inland localities on a variety of soils. Austrian and Corsican Pines are a feature of the sand dunes at Holkham, Norfolk, where they were planted between 1855 and 1890. They furnish a good object lesson of the value of the species in fixing the sand dunes and the provision of shelter. Its timber, though coarse in grain, is very durable, and useful for outside work.

At Kew Gardens, near the main gate, one can judge the value of the Corsican Pine for planting on poor, dry, sandy soil, for there are several fine trees, including an old one over ninety feet high. This tree was brought to England by Salisbury in 1814 when a seedling only six inches high.

THE STONE PINE

Family PINACEAE *Pinus pinea*

It must be confessed that the Stone Pine, with its squat, heavy, umbrella-like head, is less beautiful than picturesque, a point that strongly commends it to the landscape painter.

The date of its introduction to Britain is not known, but it has been in cultivation here certainly for nearly four hundred years. In its native countries it attains a height of sixty to eighty feet, but in this country the finest examples are about sixty feet.

Its trunk, covered with rugged, and deeply fissured thick, red-grey bark, forks at no great distance from the roots, and sends off massive spreading branches of great length.

For several years the young tree produces short single leaves, but later leaves are five or six inches long, slender, and of a bright green tint, in pairs, united at their base by a pale sheath. These leaves endure for two or three years.

The pollen-bearing flowers are crowded into a spike. The female flowers are about three-quarters of an inch long, composed of pale greenish scales.

After fertilization, these grow to a length of four to six inches, of a rugged oval form, red-brown in colour, ripening in the third year. The scales of these cones are somewhat wedge-shaped, with a stout rhomboid boss, which has a depression round the central protuberance.

The seeds, which are eaten for dessert and preserved as sweetmeats in the countries where the Stone Pine is native, are enclosed in a bony shell, and it is from this circumstance that the tree gets its name.

THE JUNIPER

Family PINACEAE   *Juniperus communis*

To appreciate the variety of forms assumed by
the Juniper according to the elevation at which it
grows, it should be seen on slopes like those of
the North Downs in Surrey—one portion of the
range at Mickleham is named Juniper Hill. In
the valleys it may be found as a small shapely tree,

Fruits of Juniper.

higher up the slopes as a pyramidal shrub, and as higher and more exposed positions are reached, the Juniper gradually dwindles to a low, shapeless bush. This, however, must not be confounded with a distinct variety to which the name *nana* has been applied; it differs from the type in having shorter and broader overlapping leaves, with curved tips.

Var. *nana* is confined to the mountains of the north of our islands, and ascends to 2,700 feet, which is 300 feet higher than is recorded of the type.

Juniper in fruit. A, flowers.

The Juniper is seldom more than a shrub a few feet in height, though it occasionally develops into a small tree from ten to twenty feet high, with a girth of five feet. It has a fibrous red bark, which flakes off like that of the Yew.

The leaves are shaped like a cobbler's awl, rigid, and end in sharp points. They have thickened margins, the upper sides concave, and they are arranged round the branches in whorls of three.

The male and female flowers are on separate trees. The male catkin may be known in May by its numerous anthers and pale yellow pollen. The female catkins will be found in the axils of the leaves, and resemble buds. The scales are fleshy, and after fertilization the upper ones slowly develop into the form of a berry, which has a few undeveloped scales as its base. They do not ripen until the following year, when they are blue-black, covered with a fine glaucous bloom. They have a pungent flavour, which is utilized in concocting gin. The " berries " have long been known as a stimulant for the kidneys.

The Virginian Juniper (*Juniperus virginiana*), or " Red Cedar " as it is called on the American continent, is a much larger plant, which is frequently seen in our parks and gardens. It varies in habit, and may be low and spreading, bush-like, or tall and tapering, thirty to forty feet high. Its leaves are in threes, like those of our native species, but the three are united by their bases. The juvenile foliage is needle-like resembling that of the Common Juniper, but the adult leaves are scale-like. Both types of leaves are found on the tree at the same time.

It is with the red heart-wood of this tree that our " cedar " pencils are covered, large quantities of the timber being imported for the purpose.

The Virginian Juniper was mentioned by John Evelyn in 1664, and is believed to have been introduced by him from North America.

LAWSON'S CYPRESS

Family PINACEAE   *Chamaecyparis lawsoniana*

Lawson's Cypress belongs to that section of Conifers which includes the Junipers, and is a representative of the North American sylva. It is a native of South-West Oregon to North-West California, where it is believed to have been first discovered by Jeffrey, about 1852. In the

United States it is known as the Port Orford Cypress.

In its native home the Lawson Cypress attains

a height of between one hundred and twenty and one hundred and fifty f e e t, occasionally reaching two hundred feet, with a b a s e circumference of forty feet. The thick brown b a r k splits into r o u n d e d s c a l y ridges. The short horizontal branches divide a good deal towards their leafy extremities, which are curved, and commonly drooping.

The leaves are l i t t l e evergreen scales, which overl a p, a n d being closely pressed to the branchlet, c o mpletely clothe and hide it. They are bright dark-green in colour, and endure for three or four years.

The male flowers are produced at the tips of the short branchlets, formed a year earlier. They are of cylindric form, crimson in colour, and each stamen bears from two to six anther-cells.

LAWSON'S CYPRESS

The small cones are more or less globular, but instead of a large number of spirally arranged overlapping scales, as in the Pines and Firs, here there are only eight, whose edges at first join to form a box. When the " cone " is ripe these scales separate, to allow the escape of the seeds.

Foliage and cones.

Lawson's Cypress produces a valuable wood, close-grained and strong, yet light. It is considered one of the most important timber trees of North America; but in this country it has been planted solely with a view to its ornamental qualities. Its perfect hardiness and its freedom of growth may, with longer experience, lead to its being regarded as a timber producer here also.

The Common Cypress (*Cupressus sempervirens*), of the Mediterranean region and the East, has been cultivated in this country for over 350 years, but it is only hardy in the south and west.

THE LARCH

Family PINACEAE   *Larix decidua*

The Larch is naturally a tree of the mountains, ascending to great elevations. Unmixed forests of Larch in the Bavarian Alps occur between 3,000 and 6,000 feet above sea-level, and on the central Swiss Alps it ascends to nearly 7,000 feet. A long winter of real cold is necessary for its full development and the ripening of its wood, and for that reason the timber of Larch grown in England is inferior to that grown in its native countries, because our winters are either short or mild, and neither gives the tree the full rest it needs.

It is a European tree, and was introduced to England at some date prior to 1629. For one hundred and fifty years it appears to have been cultivated here merely as an ornamental garden tree. Then attention was directed to its value as a timber tree, and

gold medals were offered for Larch planting and essays upon its economic importance. Already (1728) the second Duke of Atholl had begun those experiments in Larch growing for timber which have been continued by his successors on a vast scale, the fourth Duke planting on 15,000 acres of barren land no fewer than 27,000,000 Larch trees. Their example has been copied on a smaller scale all over the country.

The Larch is a lofty tree, with a very straight tapering trunk, ordinarily attaining a length between eighty and one hundred feet, but under

A, Flower.

very favourable conditions one hundred and twenty feet, with a girth of bole from six to twelve feet. The brown bark is easily separable into thin layers, and the growth of the tree causes it to split into deep longitudinal fissures. The long lower branches are spreading, with a downward tendency, and the tips turned upward again. The twigs are mostly pendulous, and bear long and slender light-green leaves, in bundles of thirty or forty. All the other families of Coniferous trees are evergreen, their leaves lasting for several years ; but at the beginning of winter the Larch leaves wither and fall, and the Larch-wood takes on a more lifeless aspect than is assumed by any of our native trees in their leafless condition. But in spring, when the fresh green leaves are just showing in spreading tufts, and the reddish-purple female flowers hang brightly from the gaunt branches, the Larch wears an entirely different appearance, and in summer the light grace of branches and foliage makes the Larch a beautiful object. That is, the trees that grow on the very outer edge of the wood, or, better still, one that has been planted as a specimen tree, where it has room to fling out its arms on all sides without touching anything, and can get the abundant light it needs.

The brown cones are egg-shaped, about an inch in length, the scales with loose edges.

The wood is very durable, and it has the great recommendation of being fit for ordinary use when the tree is only forty years old. It is most valuable for the purposes where exposure to all weathers is a necessity, for it endures constant change from wet to dry. Larch bark is used for tanning, and turpentine is a product of the tree.

Unlike most Conifers, it has the power of sending out new shoots when the branches have been removed close up to the stem.

THE SILVER FIR

Family PINACEAE *Abies alba*

It is recorded that a specimen of the Silver Fir was planted in Harefield Park, near Uxbridge, in the year 1603, and this is usually regarded as the date of its introduction to England.

The home of the Silver Fir is in the mountain regions of Central and Southern Europe. On the

Pyrenees it is found at an elevation of 6,500 feet. Specimens have been recorded in Southern Germany that have attained a height of nearly two hundred feet, but in this country a more usual stature is from one hundred to one hundred and twenty feet, with a bole girth between ten and twenty feet.

Its trunk is straight and erect, tapering gently, and covered with smooth bark, of a greyish-brown colour, which in aged specimens becomes rugged and fissured longitudinally, and of a silvery-grey colour.

Until the Silver Fir is about twelve years old its growth is slow, and its annual increase is only a few inches, but later it will be as many feet. During this early stage spring frosts often destroy the leader-shoot, but its place is taken by another shoot, and soon the symmetry of the tree is restored. It retains its lower branches for a period of forty or fifty years, but after that age they begin to fall off. Whilst the tree is growing up—which is, roughly speaking, during its first two hundred years—the crown forms a slender bush ; but its vertical growth completed, the crown grows laterally, and becomes flat-topped. Its life period covers about four hundred years. It is a deep-rooting species, with

a branching tap-root, and succeeds best in an open soil that is moist without being wet.

The leaves are flat and slender, not in bundles, as in the Scots Pine, but arranged along the branchlets in two or three dense ranks. They are dark, rich green above, about an inch long, and on the flattened underside there is a bluish-white stripe on each side of the midrib, which gives a silvery appearance to the foliage when upturned, as is usual on the fertile branches. These leaves endure from six to nine years.

The flowers appear in May at the tips of the branches. The male flowers are about three-quarters of an inch long, and consist of two or three series of overlapping scales, enclosing the yellow stamens.

The cones are cylindrical, with a blunt top, always erect, six to eight inches long, and from one and a quarter to two inches in diameter. On the back of each of the broad scales there is a long, slender, pointed bract, which extends beyond the scale and turns downward. At first these cones are green, and then become reddish, and when mature are brown ; but maturity is not reached until eighteen months after their appearance. The angular seeds are furnished with a broad wing twice their length. They are shed by the cones in the spring following their maturity, the scales falling at the same time and leaving the core of the cone on the tree.

As a rule, the tree does not produce fertile seeds until it is about forty years of age, but seedless cones are formed from its twentieth year. Although the flowers of both sexes are found on the same tree, it may be that for a series of years only cones are produced.

The timber, which has an irregular grain, is strong, and does not warp ; but it is soft, and not enduring where it is exposed to the weather. It is yellowish-white in colour, and is largely used for interior work.

THE NORWAY SPRUCE

Family PINACEAE   *Picea abies*

Although the Norway Spruce is classed among introduced species, it can lay claim to have been one of the older forest trees of Britain, for the upper beds of the Tertiary formations contain abundant evidence that the Spruce was a native here when those strata were laid down. Of its modern introduction here there is no record, but it is known that it was at some date prior to 1548. It is widely distributed as a native tree throughout the continent of Europe with the exception of Denmark and Holland, and reaches an altitude of 6,500 feet on the central Alpine ranges. It is the principal forest tree on the elevated tracts of Germany and Switzerland.

The Norway Spruce is a tall and graceful tree with tapering trunk, one hundred and twenty to one hundred and fifty feet in height, though in this country, when full-grown, it would be about eighty feet high, with a bole circumference of about nine feet. At first covered with thin, smooth, warm-brown bark, in later life this breaks up into irregular scales, thin layers of which are cast off. Instead of a bushy crown, such as seen in the Silver Fir, the Spruce ends in a delicate spire, so familiar in the Christmas-tree, which is a Norway Spruce in the nursery stage. The branches are in very regular tiers from base to summit, and the branchlets go off almost opposite each other, densely clothed with the short

grass-green needles. These are from a half to three-quarters of an inch in length, four-sided, and ending in a fine sharp point. They endure for six or seven years.

The flowers are produced near the ends of last year's shoots, those with stamens being borne singly or in clusters of two or three. They are about three-quarters of an inch in length, and of a yellow colour, tinged with pink.

The cones, which hang downwards, are almost cylindrical, about five inches long and one and a half inches in diameter. The pale-brown scales are thin, and loosely overlap. The seeds, of which there are two under each scale, are very small, with a transparent brown wing, five times the length of the seed. The flowers appear in May, and the seeds are not ripe until nearly a year later.

The tree is a shallow rooter, the roots going off horizontally in all directions a little below the surface, and becoming intimately matted with those of neighbouring trees. This surface-rooting often leads to disaster in plantations and forests of Spruce, for it is least able of all the Firs to withstand a gale, which will sometimes make a broad avenue through the plantation by toppling the trees one against another.

The wood of the Spruce, though light, is even grained, elastic and durable, and the straightness of its stem makes it very valuable for all purposes where great length and straightness are required. It supplies resin and pitch, and most newspapers and the cheaper periodicals now issued largely owe their existence to the Spruce, for its fibres reduced to pulp are made into paper upon which they are printed.

When grown in a wood the Spruce loses its lower branches early, but when given sufficient " elbow-room " these remain to a good old age, so that from spire to earth the graceful cone of bright green is continuous.

According to the International Rules we must now use the earlier name, *Picea abies* for the Spruce in preference to the better known *P. excelsa.*

THE DOUGLAS FIR

Family PINACEAE   *Pseudotsuga menziesii*

David Douglas, in his capacity of collector to the Royal Horticultural Society, landed at Fort Vancouver on the Columbia River in 1825, and not only sent home herbarium specimens, but seeds also, of this conifer. It was by means of these seeds that the Douglas Fir was introduced to Britain.

THE DOUGLAS FIR

Under the most favourable natural conditions, as around Puget Sound and on the western slopes of the Sierra Nevada, the Douglas Fir grows to a height of three hundred feet, with a girth of thirty to forty feet, but on the drier slopes of the Rocky Mountains it is not more than a hundred feet high. In Colorado, forests of Douglas Fir are found at an elevation of 11,000 feet. The tree has not been sufficiently long established in this country to say what dimensions it will reach, though it appears to have taken kindly to Ireland and to Devon and Cornwall, where the rate of growth of young trees is about thirty inches a year. There are plenty of trees in these islands, planted about the year 1834, which have reached or passed one hundred feet, and there is no doubt that towards our western coasts this height will be greatly exceeded.

The Douglas Fir is of pyramidal outline, with the lowest branches bending to the ground under their weight of branchlets and leaves ; above, they spread horizontally, but the uppermost are more or less ascending. The branchlets are given off mostly in opposite pairs, densely clothed with slender, rich green leaves three-quarters to one and a quarter inches in length, paler beneath.

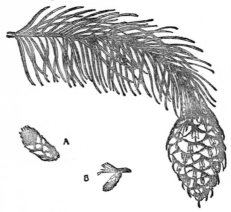

A, female flower; B, male flower.

They endure for six or seven years, and are arranged in three or four ranks.

The male flowers will be found clustered at intervals on the underside of the previous year's shoots, whilst the cones are formed at the tips of the lateral branchlets, and hang downwards. These cones are somewhat elliptical in outline, from two and a half to four inches long, with large scales, and from the back of each there extends a three-clawed bract, the middle claw or awn being very long.

The Douglas Fir produces excellent timber, and is a most valuable forest tree, not only on that account, but because of its adaptability to varying conditions of soil and climate. It is the most widely distributed of all American forest trees, and the area of its distribution is spread over thirty-two degrees of latitude, and from end to end of this range it has, in the words of Sargent, " to endure the fierce gales and long winters of the north, and the nearly perpetual sunshine of the Mexican Cordilleras ; to thrive in the rain and fog which sweep almost continuously along the Pacific coast range, and on the arid mountain slopes of the interior, where for months every year rain never falls." It appears to thrive best where the air is humid and the soil well drained.

It begins to bear cones about its twenty-fifth year.

Its suitability for masts and spars will be evident to all visitors to the Royal Botanic Gardens at Kew. The flagstaff set up in the gardens is from the bole of a Douglas Fir. The pole is 214 feet long with a diameter of 33 inches at the base, tapering to 12 inches at the top and weighing about 18 tons. It was brought from Vancouver Island and was erected in 1919 to replace a smaller spar of the same species.

The full life of the Douglas Fir is estimated to be about 750 years.

THE CEDAR OF LEBANON

Family PINACEAE   *Cedrus libani*

The Cedar varies greatly—no tree more so—in height and general outline, according to situation and environment, and though well-grown trees in this country may be stated as from fifty to eighty feet, we have examples of one hundred and one hundred and twenty feet where the conditions have been specially favourable. But the Cedar, as usually seen on lawns and in parks, has a low, rounded, or flattened top, the great spreading arms having grown more rapidly than the trunk. Thus grown, the huge bole has seldom any great length, throwing out these timber branches at from six to ten feet from the ground, and immediately afterwards the trunk is divided into several stems. From these the main branches take a curving direction, at first ascending, but the part farthest from the trunk becoming almost horizontal. It is chiefly at the extremity of the branches that the branchlets and leaves are produced.

The evergreen leaves last for three, four, or five years, and are needle-shaped, varying about an inch in length. They are produced in tufts that are arranged spirally round dwarf shoots, mostly on the upper side of the branchlets.

The male flowers are to be found at the extremity of branchlets which, though six or seven years old, are very short, their development having been arrested.

The solid, purple-brown cones are only three or four inches long, broad-topped, and with a diameter of half the length ; the scales thin and closely pressed together ; they are at first greyish-green, tinged with pink. The development and maturity of these cones take two or three seasons,

and they remain on the tree for several years
longer. The seeds are angular, with a wedge-
shaped wing.

The trees do not produce cones until they are
from twenty-five to thirty years old; but they
may be a hundred years old before producing
either male or female flowers.

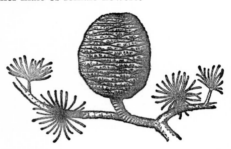

The trunk is covered with thick, rough, deeply
fissured bark. On the branches the bark is
smooth, and peels off in thin flakes.

The Cedar, in its native habitat, produces
admirable timber, but that of trees grown in this
country is described as reddish-white, light and
spongy, easily worked, but very apt to shrink and
warp, and by no means durable. For these
reasons the tree is grown almost solely for
ornament.

THE DEODAR OR INDIAN CEDAR

Family PINACEAE   *Cedrus deodara*

Although the differences between the Cedar of
Lebanon and the Deodar are really slight, they
are sufficient at once to strike the ordinary
observer. In proportion to the height of the
trunk, for example, the main branches are much
shorter, the result being a more regular pyramidal

outline, terminating in a light spire. The terminal shoots of the branches are longer, more slender, and quite pendulous. There is no

necessity, therefore, for repeating the particulars already given respecting the Cedar of Lebanon, which apply to the Deodar with such modifications as are indicated above.

The headquarters of the Deodar are in the mountains of north-west India, where it forms forests at various altitudes above 3,500 feet. Its vertical distribution extends to a height of 12,000 feet, but its principal habitat lies between 6,000 and 10,000 feet.

Deodar timber produced in its native forests is exceedingly durable, being compact and even grained, not liable to warp or split, and standing the test of being alternately wet and dry.

THE DEODAR OR INDIAN CEDAR

It is to the Hon. W. L. Melville that we are indebted for the introduction of the Deodar to Britain in 1831, and during the next ten years many young trees were raised here from seeds. Favourably impressed by the rapidity of growth of these seedlings, large numbers of Deodar seeds

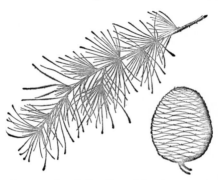

were imported and distributed by the government, and high estimates were formed of the future value of these trees. But in framing these estimates one important factor was omitted—the uncertainty of the British climate, with its rapid changes. A score or two of years served to demonstrate that such conditions were opposed to the longevity and uniform development that produced sound timber on the Indian mountains. In spite of this failure, there are to be seen in many parts of these islands fine young Deodars of forty or fifty years, and from fifty to seventy feet in height.

THE CHILE PINE

Family PINACEAE   *Araucaria araucana*

The Chile Pine, or "Monkey Puzzle," is a native of Southern Chile. It forms extensive pine forests in the province of Arauco, from which it gets its name, and to whose inhabitants the seeds are a most important item of their food-supply. Not only do the trees in these forests lose their

lower branches, but even those growing in the
open plains of their native country have similarly
bare trunks for nearly half their height. It is
therefore a satisfaction to know that the finest
specimens grown in this country have really sur-
passed those grown in their natural home.

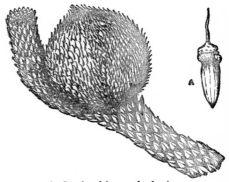

A, Seed, with attached wing.

The height reached by old trees is from eighty
to one hundred feet, with a trunk-girth of from
sixteen to twenty-three feet. The tapering of this
trunk is very slight, and a few of the stiff, spine-
tipped leaves, with which its younger extremity is
densely clothed, still remain attached in a dried-up
condition far down the column. These leaves
will have been observed to cover the branches
entirely, not being restricted, as in most trees,
to the newly-formed branchlets and twigs. They
are very hard and endure for about fifteen years;

are about an inch and a quarter long, and overlap, though their sharp-pointed ends turn away from the branch.

The cylindrical male flowers are four or five inches long, borne singly or in small clusters. The sexes are usually on separate trees, but some individuals produce flowers of both kinds. The female flowers are about four inches long, almost round in shape, but broader at the base than above. They are covered with long, narrow, overlapping scales, beneath which are found the seeds when the flower has developed into the brown cone, which is six inches in diameter. The scales are then easily detached ; in fact, when the seeds are ripe, the cone falls to pieces. The winged seed is about an inch and a half long, enclosed in a hard thin shell.

The Chile Pine does not succeed in this country unless it is given pure air, sunshine, abundant moisture, and a well-drained subsoil. It will grow to a very handsome tree if these conditions are observed.

INDEX

INDEX